JAPANESE KANJI
MNEMONICS
RADICALS

JAPANESE KANJI MNEMONICS RADICALS

Lindsay Jimenez

Dioxelis Lopez

2026

ACKNOWLEDGEMENTS

To my followers and fellow learners: this is for you. Much has changed in the six years since my first book, but your unwavering support has been the one constant. Your curiosity and encouragement are the "radicals" that built this project. Writing this has been a profound privilege, and I am deeply grateful for the opportunity to help you navigate the beautiful complexity of the Japanese language.

"Thank you for being the 'power' (力) behind my work."

 Book design by Lindsay Jimenez

Cover design by Harold Jimenez

 Formatting by Dioxelis Lopez

Ancient script images: xiaoxue.iis.sinica.edu.tw

HOW TO USE THIS BOOK

The goal of this book is to transform your Japanese study from a struggle of rote memorization into a process of logical decoding. In my years of studying Japanese, I discovered a "cheat code": **Prioritizing radicals over individual characters.** When you master the 93 radicals in this book, you aren't just learning 93 shapes—you are learning the components that make up over 90% of all daily-use *kanji*. This approach significantly increases your learning speed and retention.
Prerequisite: Although not totally required, this book is ideal for students who have already mastered **Hiragana** and **Katakana**.

Each radical is presented in a two-part layout to engage both your analytical brain and your visual memory.

1. The Front Page: Context & Evolution

- **History & Etymology:** We begin with the "Why." You will explore the ancient pictographic roots of the radical. Understanding that a radical was originally a "gate," a "knife," or a "kneeling person" creates a mental anchor that makes it impossible to forget.

- **Categories & Examples:** We show you exactly where this radical "lives." You will see how it behaves in real characters, categorized by meaning (e.g., "Actions," "Location," or "Nature").

2. The Back Page: Memory & Practice

- **Mnemonics:** We provide memory aids. These are designed for prompt memorization, linking the ancient shape to the modern form through a simple shape.

- **Stroke Order:** Precision matters. This section shows the correct sequence for writing the radical, ensuring your *kanji* look balanced and professional.

- **Writing Exercise:** Muscle memory is the final step. Use this dedicated space to practice the radical until the movement becomes second nature.

This book is a companion, not a silo. To get the most out of these 93 building blocks, I recommend the following:

- **The "Spotting" Game:** Once you study a radical, look for it in the wild! Whether you are reading a manga, a news article, or a restaurant menu, try to identify the "mini-stories" within the complex *kanji* you see.

- **Context is King:** The best way to cement these radicals in your mind is to see them used in actual *kanji* during your daily vocabulary studies.

- **Review Regularly:** Don't just move forward. Flip back to the early radicals occasionally to ensure the "foundations" are still rock solid.

By the time you reach the end of this book, you won't just be reading Japanese—you'll be understanding its DNA.

93
MOST COMMON RADICALS

一	彳	米
亠	幺	糸
亻	心	罒
儿	戈	羊
八	戸	羽
冖	扌	肉
冫	攵	舟
刂	方	艹
力	斤	虫
十	日	衤
卩	月	耳
厂	木	虍
又	欠	行
口	止	見
囗	歹	言
土	殳	貝
夕	氵	足
大	牛	車
女	犭	邑
子	火	酉
宀	王	金
寸	田	門
小	广	阜
尸	皿	隹
辶	目	雨
山	石	頁
工	礻	食
巾	禾	馬
广	穴	鬼
弓	立	魚
彡	竹	鳥

RADICAL NAMES
BASED ON POSITION
HEN
私
TSUKURI
利
KANMURI
安
ASHI
児
TARE
病
NYOU
道
KAMAE
回

ONE 一

The radical for **"one"** (一) is the most essential of all components. It is the simplest character in terms of stroke count, but it is a powerful philosophical symbol representing unity, a beginning, or a physical boundary.

Known in Japanese simply as いち (*ichi*), this character is a pure pictogram. In its most primitive form, it represents a single finger or a tally stick used for counting. Beyond the number "one," it represents a horizontal plane—the horizon, a floor, or a ceiling—that provides a reference point for everything else.

When 一 acts as a radical, it usually organizes *kanji* into these two categories:

1. **Numerical & Measurement:**

   - 万 (まん – ten thousand): It uses the horizontal line as a base for a large number.

2. **Positional Reference (The Horizon):** The line acts as a "ground" or "sky" to show where things are located.

   - 上 (うえ – up/above): A mark placed **above** the horizontal line.

   - 下 (した – down/below): A mark placed **below** the horizontal line.

ONE

Try it:

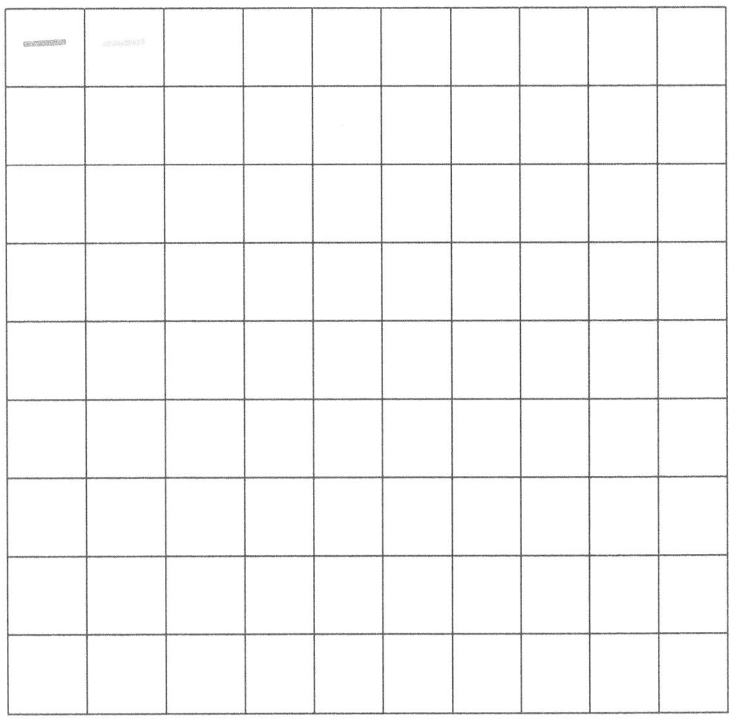

LID 亠

The radical for **"lid"** (亠) is a unique symbol that acts as a structural "cap" for many *kanji*. It is often the source of confusion for beginners because it looks similar to other radicals, but its specific placement and history make it distinct.

In Japanese, this radical is famously known as **なべぶた** (*nabebuta*), which literally translates to **"pot lid."** In ancient scripts, it represented the highest point of an object. This could be the **lid** of a container, the **roof** of a tower, or even the **crown** of a human head.

When 亠 acts as a radical, it typically organizes *kanji* into two main categories:

1. **Architecture and High Structures:**

   - 亭 (てい – pavilion/inn): Depicts a tall, tiered building with a roof on top.

   - 京 (きょう – capital/metropolis): Originally represented a tall building in a large city.

2. **The Human Head or Top:**

   - 交 (まじわる – to intersect/exchange): This is actually a pictogram of a person with their legs crossed; the 亠 at the top represents the **head**.

   - 亡 (なくなる – deceased): The head of the person who passed away.

LID

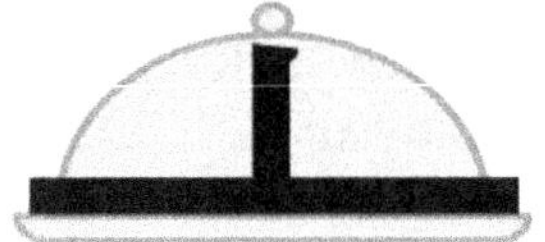

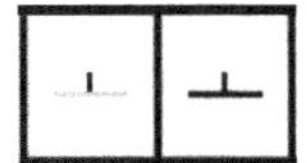

Try it:

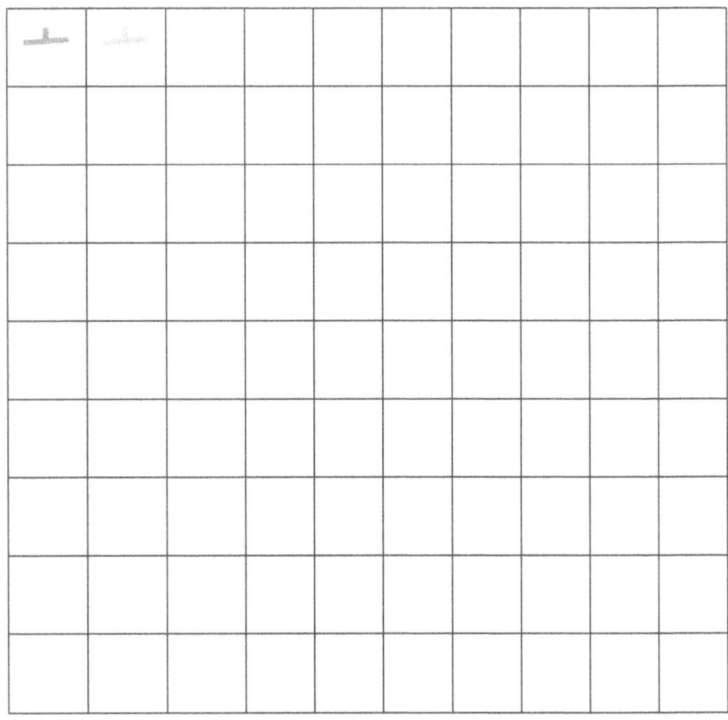

PERSON 人 亻

The radical for **"person"** (人) is a powerhouse of the Japanese writing system. It appears in hundreds of *kanji*, and once you recognize its different "disguises," you will be able to guess the meaning of many new words.

This radical is one of the most famous pictograms. It depicts the profile of a **standing person**. In ancient forms, you could see a person bowing slightly or walking, showing the legs and the torso. It now represents anything related to human beings: their physical bodies, their social roles, their occupations, and their behaviors.

This radical has **two primary forms**:

- 人 **(ひと)**: This form can stand alone as a *kanji* meaning **"person."**
- 亻 **(にんべん)**: This is the **simplified, most common variant form** of the radical.

When 人 or 亻 acts as a radical, it typically indicates:

1. **Humans:** a person, body, or physical attributes.

   - 仙 (せん – Hermit): A **person** (亻) far away in a mountain (山).

   - 体 (からだ – Body): A **person** (亻) and their **foundation/roots** (本).

2. **Actions performed by humans:**

   - 休 (やすむ – to rest): A **person** (亻) leaning against a **tree** (木).

PERSON

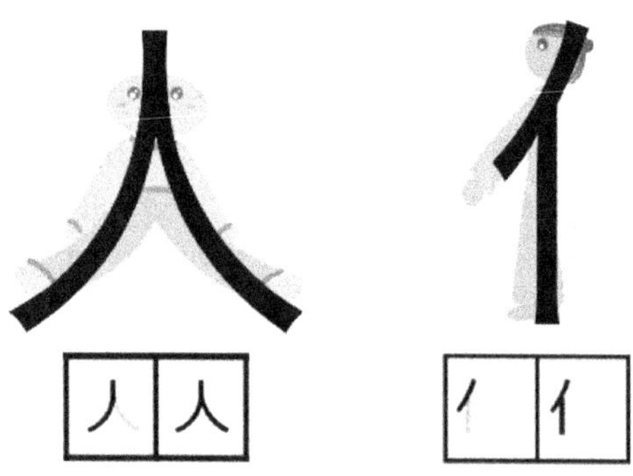

Try it:

LEGS 儿

The radical for **"human legs"** (儿) is a fundamental building block in Japanese. Known as **ひとあし** (*hitoashi* - "human legs") or **にんにょう** (*ninnyou* - "human legs on the bottom"), it acts as a pedestal. Whether it represents a child, a leader, or an ancestor, this radical usually indicates a human being in a specific state or position.

The shape is a minimalist sketch of a human figure from the waist down. It consists of two strokes representing the legs. The left stroke is usually straight or slightly curved, while the right stroke often has a "hook" or a "flick," suggesting the foot or the forward motion of a step.

When 儿 appears, it usually walks the character into one of these two categories:

1. **Human Identity and Roles:**

    - 兄 (あに – older brother): A **mouth** (口) on top of **legs** (儿). This represents the "spokesman" or the one who speaks for the family.

    - 児 (じ – child/infant): A simplified version of an old character showing a child's head.

2. **Origins and Movement:**

    - 先 (さき – before/ahead): This depicts a **foot** moving forward over **legs** (儿). It means to be "ahead" in time or space (as in 先生 - teacher).

LEGS

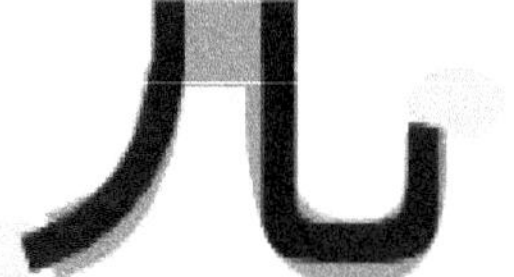

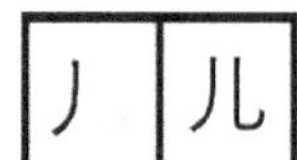

Try it:

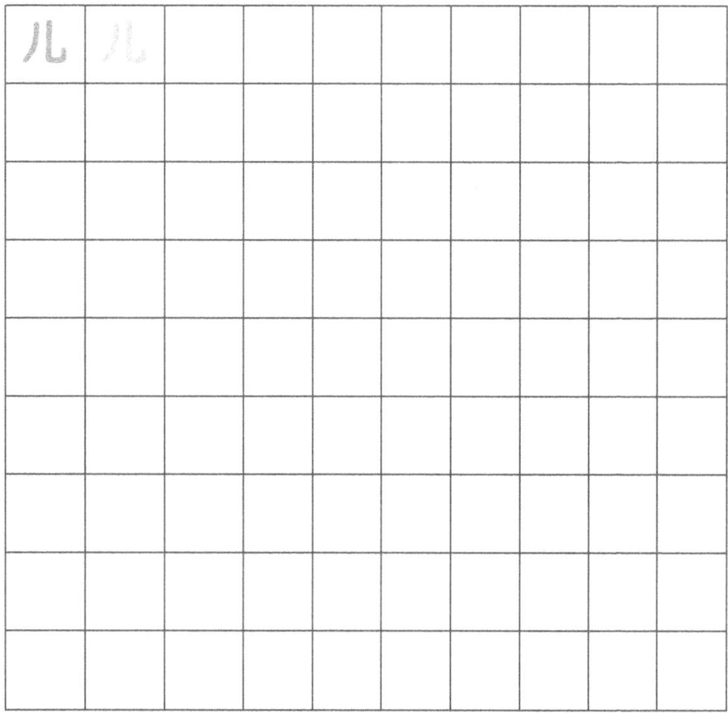

EIGHT 八

The radical for **"eight"** (八) is a deceptively simple component. While we know it today as a number, its origins are rooted in **action**. It represents the separation of a whole into parts, marking characters that involve splitting, sharing, or distribution.

Known in Japanese as はち (*hachi*), this radical is a minimalist pictogram of divergence. It consists of two strokes that curve away from each other. Unlike the character for "human" (人) or "enter" (入), the two strokes of 八 **do not touch** at the top. The gap between the lines represents a central point that has been forced open or divided. It is the visual shorthand for "away from the center."

When 八 appears, it usually categorizes the character into one of these two themes:

1. **Separation and Distribution:**

    -   公 (こう – public/official): Originally meant to **divide** (八) and distribute private goods to the community.

2. **Soldiers and Tools:**

    -   兵 (へい – soldier): The bottom 八 represents the hands or the base of a soldier holding a heavy **tool**.

    -   具 (ぐ – tool): To hold an object with **both hands** (represented by the 八 at the bottom).

EIGHT

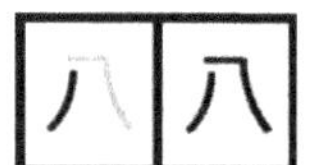

Try it:

COVER 冖

The radical for **"cover"** (冖) represents the act of concealment, wrapping, or containment. It is an essential component that defines the "space" or the "state" of the objects tucked beneath it.

Known in Japanese as **わかんむり** (*wakanmuri*), this radical is a pictogram based on a piece of cloth hanging downwards. Unlike the "Roof" radical, which implies a solid building with a chimney, this represents a simpler, more flexible covering—like a veil, a lid, or a shroud.

When 冖 appears in a character, it generally falls into one of these two categories:

1. **Physical Covering:** Direct references to items worn on the head or placed over objects.

    - 冠 (かんむり – crown/best): Represents a formal head covering.

2. **Darkness and Hiddenness:** Because a cover blocks light, it often implies things that "in the dark."

    - 冥 (めい – dark/underworld): This depicts something covered and hidden from sight.

    - 冤 (えん – injustice/false charge): Literally a "rabbit" (兎) under a "cover" (冖), suggesting someone trapped or hidden away unfairly.

COVER

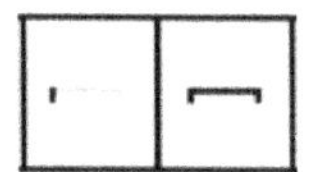

Try it:

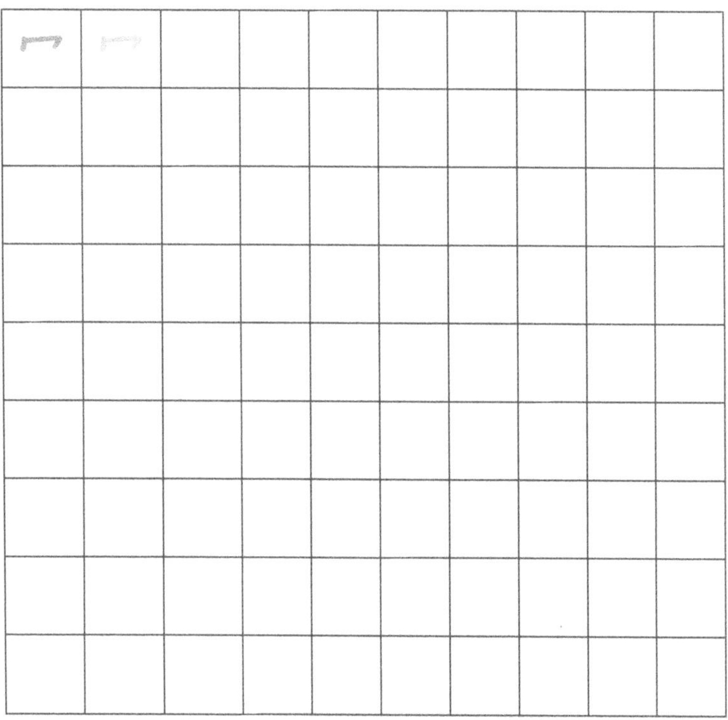

ICE 冫

The radical for **"ice"** (冫) is the essential marker for coldness, freezing, and solidifying. It represents the transition of matter from a liquid to a solid state and is the primary indicator of low temperature in the *kanji* world.

Known in Japanese as にすい (nisui), the original character was 仌, a pictogram of ice crystals or layers of ice found in a frozen river. It consists of two short strokes. The top stroke is a short diagonal, and the bottom stroke is a sharp upward flick. It represents the "cracks" or "facets" of a frozen surface.

When 冫 appears, it chills the meaning of the character into one of these three categories:

1. **Temperature and Physical Sensation:**

   - 冷 (つめたい – cold/chilly): **Ice** (冫) plus a "command/order" (令). Think of the sharp, commanding bite of cold air.

2. **Freezing and State Changes:**

   - 凍 (こおる – to freeze)

   - 凝 (こる – to freeze/coagulate)

3. **Seasonal and Time:**

   - 冬 (ふゆ – winter)

ICE

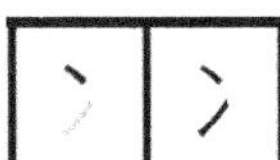

Try it:

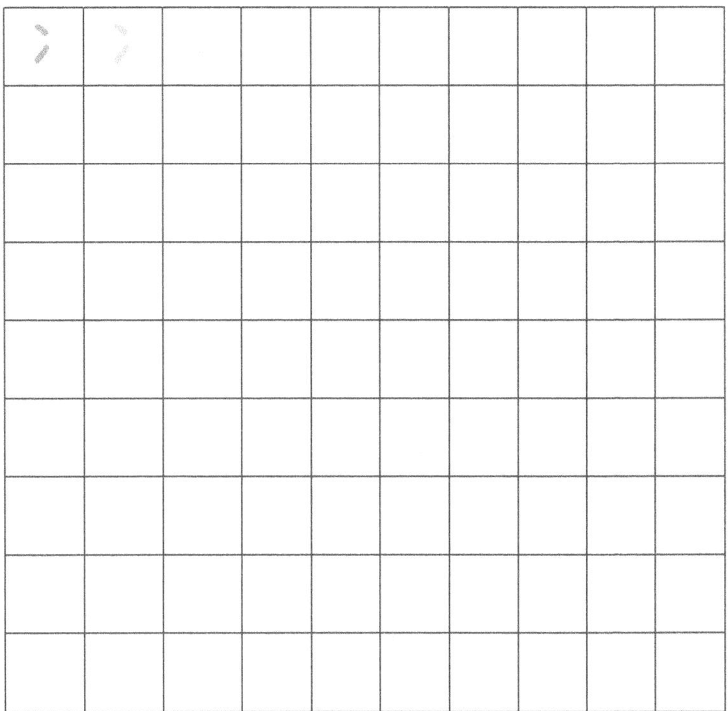

KNIFE 刀 刂

The radical for **"knife"** (刀 / 刂) is essential for recognizing *kanji* related to tools and actions involving division or cutting. This radical is derived from an ancient pictogram that resembled a **knife** (刀).

 The "knife" radical has **two primary forms**:

1. **刀 (かたな):**

    - This form can stand alone as a *kanji* meaning "**sword**" or "**saber**" (like a samurai sword). When used as a radical, it is typically found on the **bottom** or **right** side of a *kanji*.

2. **刂 (りっとう):**

    - This is the **simplified, variant form** of the radical. It is also the most common version and is almost always positioned on the **right side** of a *kanji*.

When this radical is found in a kanji, it signals a meaning in one of the following two categories:

1. **Actions that knives perform:**

    - 切 (きる – to cut)

    - 刻 (きざむ – To cut fine)

2. **Blades or swords:**

    - 刀 (かたな – Saber)

KNIFE

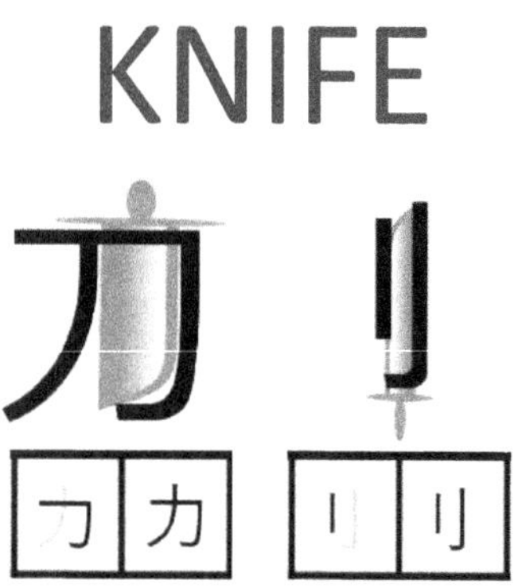

Try it:

FORCE 力

The radical for **"power"** (力) is a cornerstone of characters involving action, ability, and results. It bridges the gap between physical muscle and the tools we use to shape the world. Whether it's the effort of a student or the strength of a motor, this radical provides the "push."

 Known in Japanese as ちから (chikara), its origin is one of the most debated in linguistics, but both theories point to the same thing: **exertion.**

Theory A (The Arm): It represents a **flexed arm** with the bicep bulging, showing raw physical strength.

Theory B (The Plough): It represents an ancient **wooden plough** being pushed into the earth.

When 力 appears, it usually fuels the character with one of these three themes:

1. **Strength and Physical Ability:**

   - 勇 (ゆう – courage)

   - **力 (ちから – Strength):** The stand-alone kanji.

2. **Effort, Labor, and Persuasion:**

   - 勉 (べん – to exert/study)

3. **Merit and Result:**

   - 功 (こう – merit/success): The **power** (力) used to complete a "work/task" (工).

FORCE

Try it:

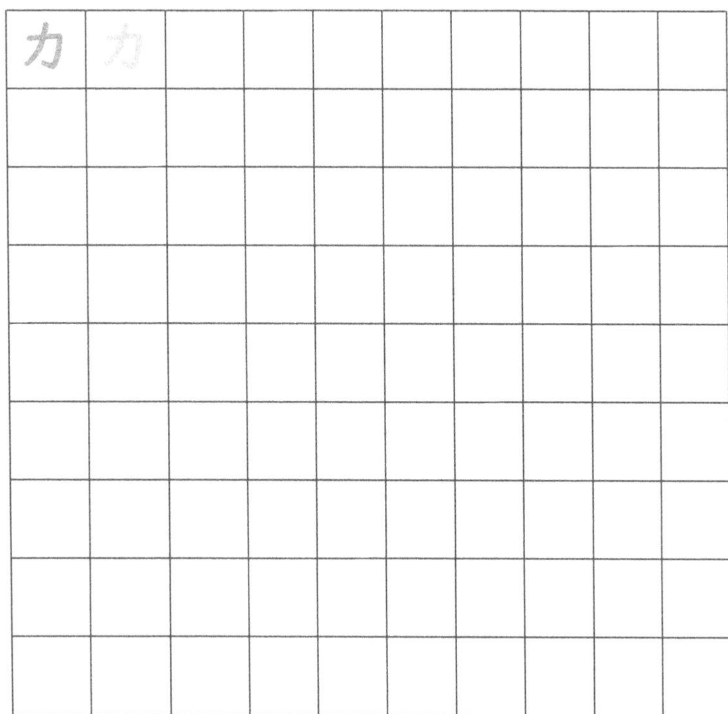

TEN 十

The radical for **"ten"** (十) is a simple but powerful component. While it is most famous for its literal meaning as a number, its role as a radical often carries a deeper symbolic weight.

Known in Japanese as じゅう (*juu*), it began as a simple **vertical stroke**. Over time, a **bulge** or a small dot was added to the middle of the line serving as a tally mark. This addition transformed the tally into a symbol for **completeness** or **fullness**.

When 十 appears as a radical, it often moves beyond the number ten to suggest one of these three categories:

1. **Numbers (in general):** Becoming the base for other numbers.

   - 千 (せん – thousand)

2. **Sufficiency:** The idea of having "enough."

   - 協 (きょう – cooperation): literally "many (十) strengths (力) working together"

3. **The Four Directions:** Because of its cross shape, it can sometimes represent universality or the four cardinal points.

   - 南 (みなみ – South)

TEN

Try it:

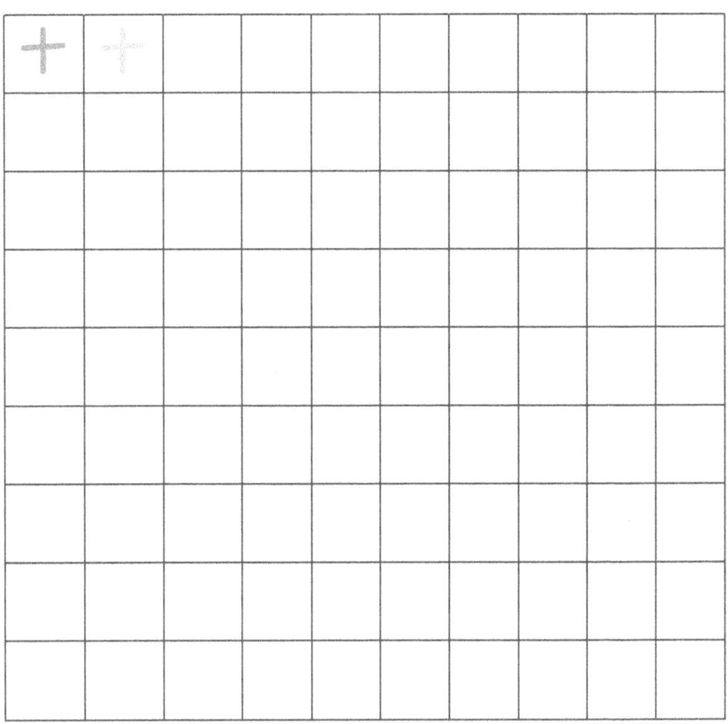

SEAL / KNEEL 卩

The radical **"seal"** (卩) is a fascinating piece of history hidden in plain sight. While it might look like a simple hook today, it originally represented a **kneeling human figure**.

 In ancient China, kneeling was the standard posture for daily life, symbolizing **respect, and submission.**

- **Standing vs. Kneeling:** This radical shares an ancestor with the "person" radical (人). However, while 人 represents a person standing up, 卩 specifically depicts someone kneeling.

- **The "Seal" Connection:** Over time, this radical became known as the **"seal"** radical 節旁 (*fushidukuri*). This is because official seals were symbols of authority—much like a kneeling person shows submission to authority.

When 卩 acts as a radical, you can observe the kneeling connection as follows:

- 印 (しるし – seal/stamp): depicting a hand pressing down on a kneeling person.

- 即 (そく – immediately): Originally showing a person kneeling down to eat a meal.

- 危 (あぶない – dangerous): Depicting a person kneeling in fear on the edge of a cliff.

SEAL / KNEEL

Try it:

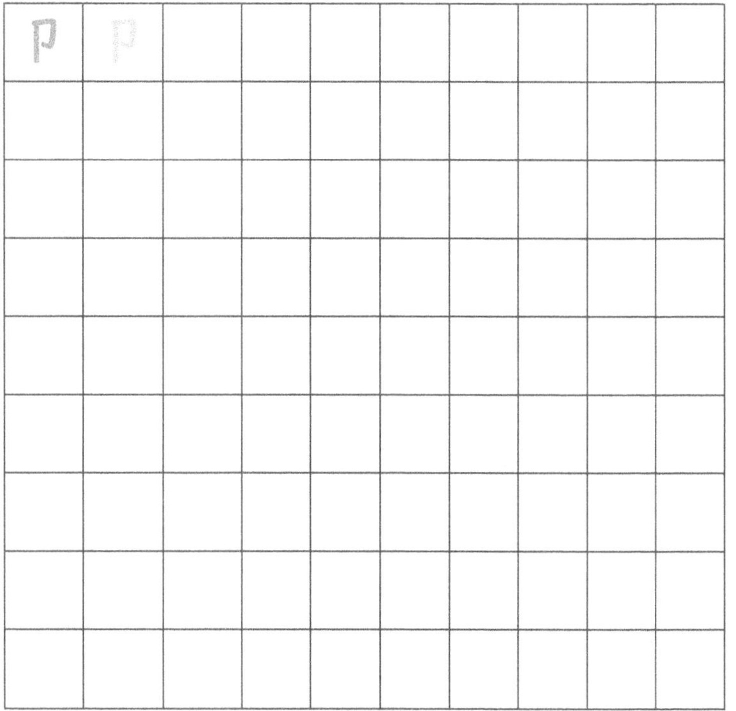

CLIFF 厂

The radical for **"cliff"** (厂) is one of the most literal pictographs in the Japanese writing system. Historically, this radical captures a piece of human history—referring to the era when people used the space beneath protruding rocks as natural shelters or dwellings.

Known in Japanese as がんだれ (gandare), the shape of 厂 represents a **jagged cliff face**. The **horizontal line** represents the protruding cliff top or an overhanging ledge. The **sloping vertical line** represents the steep wall of the mountain.

Consequently, when 厂 appears in a *kanji*, it usually signals a meaning related to one of these three categories:

1. **Obstacles or rugged terrain:**

   - 厄 (やく – misfortune/unlucky): Depicting a person trapped under a cliff.

   - 厚 (あつ・い – thick)

2. **Cliffs or rocks:**

   - 崖 (がけ – cliff)

3. **Sheltered dwellings:**

   - 厨 (ちゅう – Kitchen)

CLIFF

Try it:

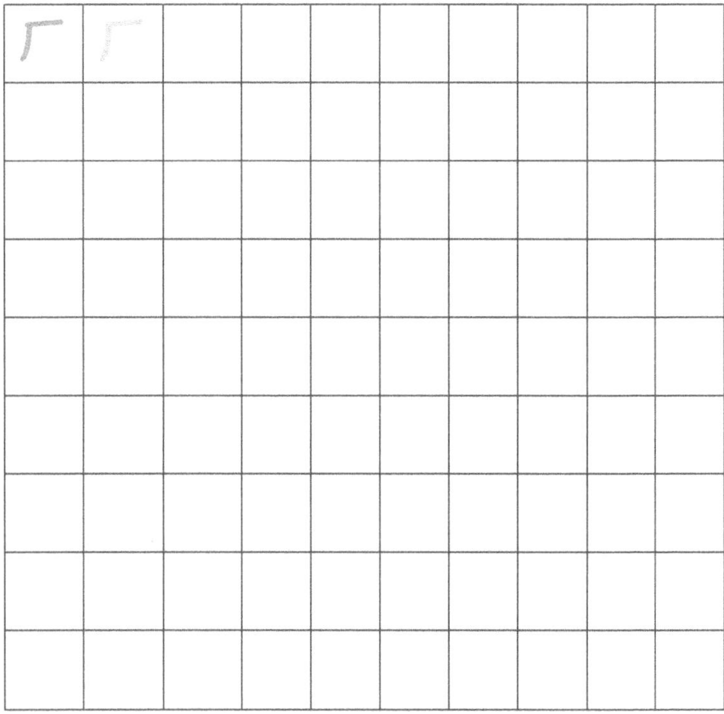

RIGHT HAND 又

The radical for **"right hand"** (又) is a fascinating example of how a character's meaning can change over thousands of years. To modern learners, the *kanji* 又 (また) is most famous for meaning **"again"**. However, when it acts as a radical, you should almost always think of it as a **right hand**.

Originally, this was a clear drawing of a hand. The top strokes represented **three fingers** (three being shorthand for "many" in ancient script), while the stroke curving to the left represented the **wrist and arm**.

Why "Again"? Linguists believe that because we use our right hand repeatedly, the "hand" symbol eventually became an abstract way to say "again."

Because this radical represents a hand, it often appears in one of these two categories:

1. **Physical actions:**

   - 取 (とる – to take): A hand (又) taking an ear (耳). In ancient times, taking the ear of a fallen enemy was a way to keep count.

   - 受 (うける – to receive): Represents two hands passing an object between them.

2. **Relationships:**

   - 友 (とも – friend): Originally depicted two hands (又) reaching out to help one another.

RIGHT HAND

又

Try it:

MOUTH 口

With over 80 kanjis containing the **"mouth"** radical, 口 (く
ち) is one of the most essential components to master.

The "mouth" radical is a pure pictogram. While it is
a perfect square today, its ancient forms were
more organic, resembling a **bowl with upturned
corners** or a pair of **smiling lips**.

What makes this radical particularly beginner-friendly is its
consistency. Unlike some radicals that change meaning
when they become a kanji, 口 almost always retains its
core meaning of "**mouth**" or "**opening.**"

When you see 口 in a character, it generally points to one
of two categories:

1. **Speech & Communication:** Actions involving the
   mouth, such as calling, singing, or shouting.

   - 叫 (さけぶ – shout/yell): Note the mouth at on
     the left!

   - 名 (な – name): A mouth 口 identifying a
     person in the evening 夕 when it's too dark to
     see them.

2. **Eating & Survival:** Physical consumption or the
   number of "mouths" to feed.

   - 味 (あじ – flavor): Related to eating.

MOUTH

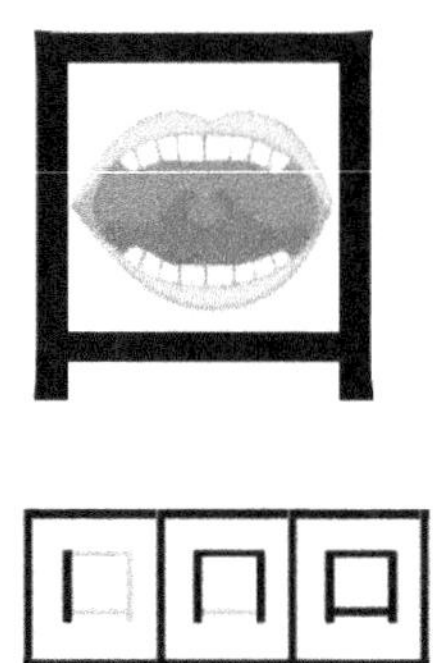

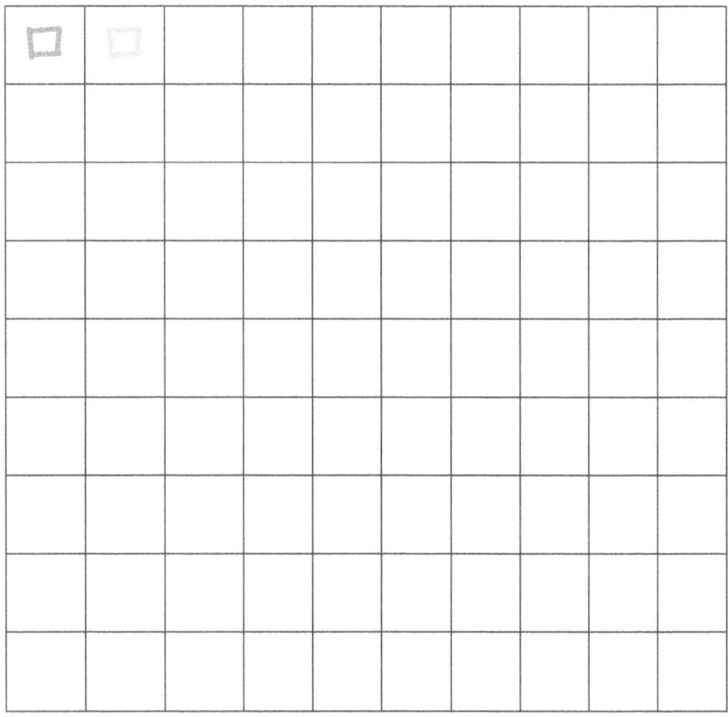

Try it:

ENCLOSURE 囗

The radical for **"enclosure"** (囗) is often the "big brother" to the mouth radical (口). While they look identical in isolation, they serve very different purposes.

The most important rule for a learner is to look at the **size and contents**:

- **The Enclosure:** It is always larger and **surrounds** other components. It acts like a fence or a border.
- **The Mouth:** It is smaller and usually sits to the side or at the bottom.

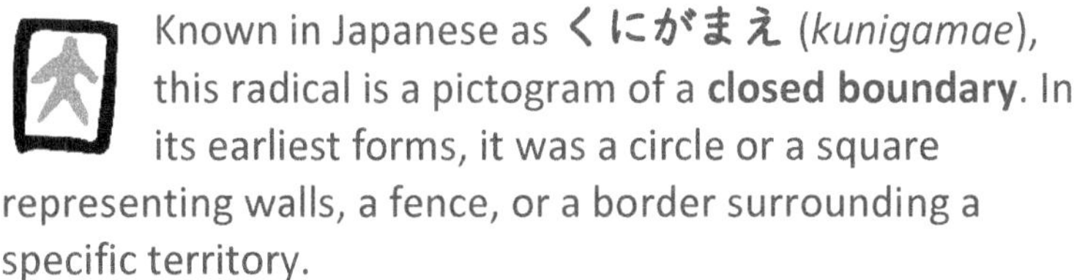 Known in Japanese as くにがまえ (*kunigamae*), this radical is a pictogram of a **closed boundary**. In its earliest forms, it was a circle or a square representing walls, a fence, or a border surrounding a specific territory.

When you see 囗 wrapping around another character, the meaning usually falls into one of these two categories:

1. **Territory and Borders:**

   - 国 (くに – country): Represents a kingdom or territory protected by a border.

2. **Imprisonment and Restriction:**

   - 囚 (しゅう – prisoner): Literally a person (人) inside an enclosure (囗).

ENCLOSURE

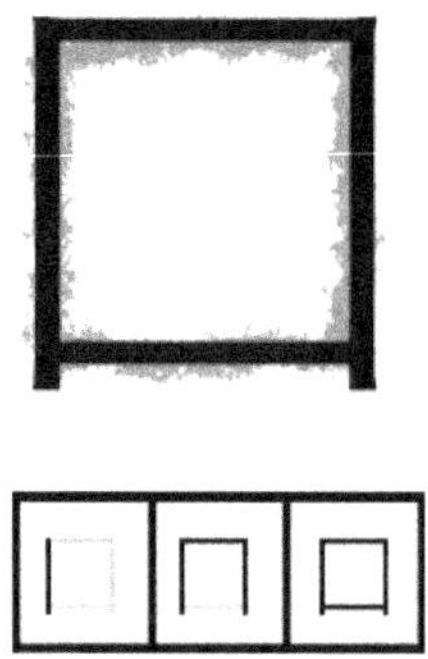

Try it:

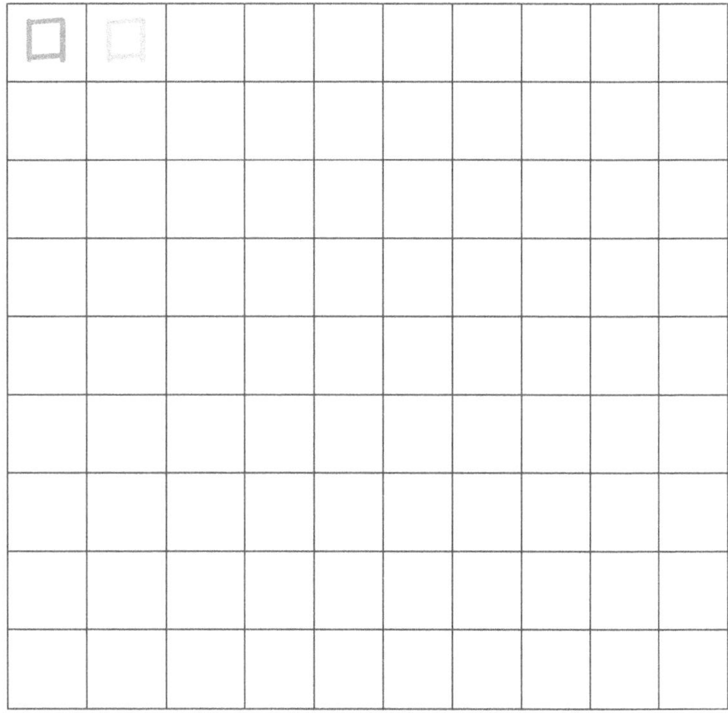

SOIL 土

The radical for **"earth"** or **"soil"** (土) is an ancient character with deep roots in philosophy and daily life. It represents the very ground we walk on and serves as a building block for many common *kanji*.

Known as つち (*tsuchi*), this radical is a pictogram of a **mound of earth** rising from the ground. Early versions showed a pointed heap of soil on a horizontal base. Over time, the bottom line was lengthened to emphasize the idea of a solid **foundation** or the vastness of the land.

When you see 土 as a radical, the *kanji* usually falls into one of two categories:

1. **Natural Terrain:** Words related to the physical land, soil, or geography.

   - 坂 (さか – hill/slope)

   - 地 (ち – ground/earth)

2. **Construction and Territory:** Historically, walls, homes, and boundaries were made of packed earth. This radical appears in words for architecture and places.
   - 城 (しろ – castle)

   - 場 (ば – place/location)

SOIL

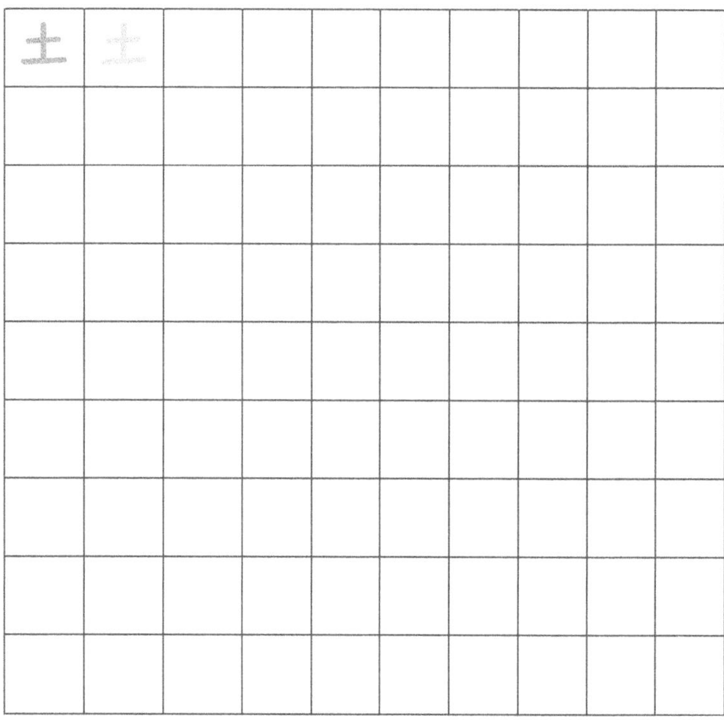

Try it:

EVENING 夕

The radical for **"evening"** (夕) is a poetic component that captures the transition from day to night. It is a staple in *kanji* related to time, darkness, and the activities that happen after the sun sets.

Known in Japanese as or **ゆうべ** (*yuube*), this radical is a pictogram originally derived from the character for **"moon"** (月). In ancient times, 夕 and 月 were actually the same character! To help distinguish them as the writing system evolved:

- **The Moon (月):** A horizontal line was added.

- **The Evening (夕):** The character remained "hollower," eventually settling on just one diagonal stroke to represent a sliver of the moon appearing at dusk.

When 夕 acts as a radical, it typically points to **nighttime**. You can see its influence in characters such as:

- 夢 (ゆめ – Dream): An activity that primarily occurs during sleep at night.

- 外 (そと – Outside): Historically, it combined "evening" (夕) and "divination/fortune telling" (卜). In ancient times, rituals performed at night were considered "outside" the normal daily order.

EVENING

Try it:

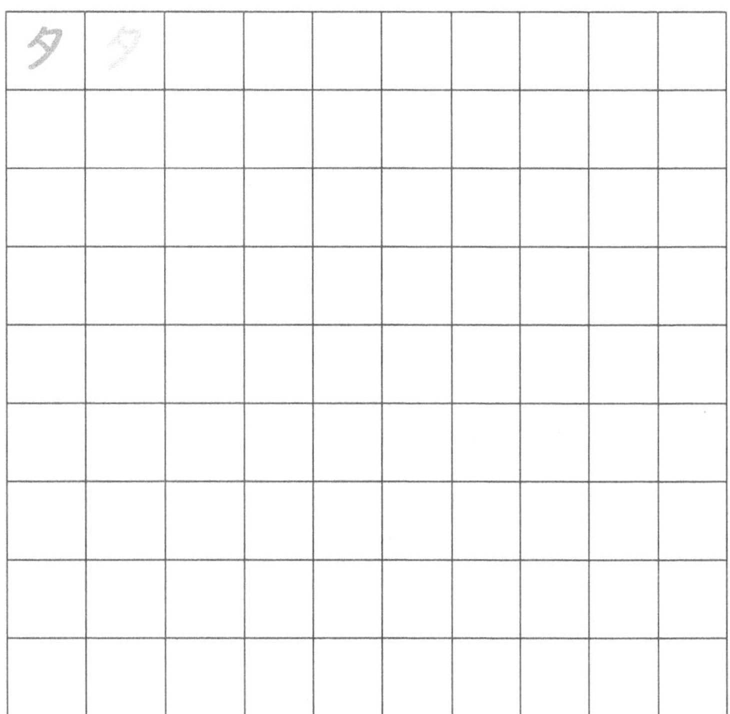

BIG 大

The radical for **"big"** (大) is one of the most recognizable and frequently used components in the Japanese language. It is essentially a visual expansion of the radical for "person" (人), making it very easy for students to remember.

Known in Japanese as だい (dai), the radical big shows a person standing tall with their **arms stretched out wide**. By extending their arms, the person occupies as much visual space as possible, symbolizing **"hugeness"** or **"greatness."** To the ancients, the human adult was the ultimate measure of all things; therefore, a fully grown adult standing at their full height was the most direct representation of "big."

When 大 appears, it usually points to one of these two categories:

1. **Size and space:**

   - 天 (てん – heaven): It's a "big" person (大) with a line above their head, representing the vast sky above us.

2. **Physical characteristics:**

   - 夫 (おっと – husband): This is a "big" person with a hairpin (一), signifying they have reached adulthood and are ready for marriage.

   - 太 (ふとい – fat/thick): It's like 大, but with a "drop" added. Think of it as "extra" big!

BIG

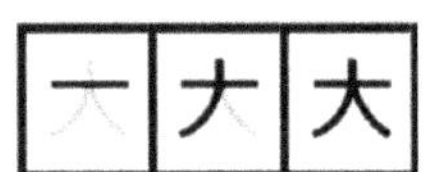

Try it:

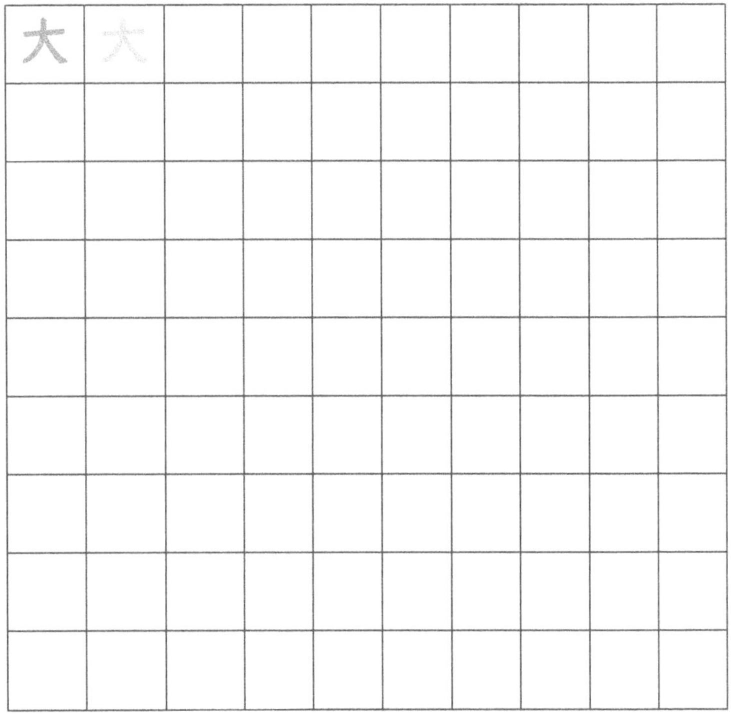

WOMAN 女

The radical for **"woman"** (女) is one of the most foundational components in Japanese. It acts as both a common stand-alone *kanji* and a radical that appears in hundreds of other characters.

Known in Japanese as **おんな** (*onna*), this radical is a pictogram of a person kneeling with their hands folded respectfully over their abdomen. Historically, this posture represented the "gentle" or "reserved" traits traditionally associated with women in ancient society. It captures a moment of quiet strength and focus on the family.

Many of the most common *kanji* containing 女 relate to family or beginnings:

- 妹 (いもうと – Younger sister): This combines "woman" (女) with "not yet" (未). It literally translates to a **not-yet-grown woman**."

- 姉 (あね – Older sister): This combines "woman" (女) with "market/city" (市). A common way to remember this is that the older sister was the one trusted to go to the market or manage the city affairs for the family.

- 始 (はじめる – To begin): This likely relates to a woman giving the "beginning" of life.

However, there are also ancient origins of some characters (like "jealousy" 嫉 or "slave" 奴) that reflect old-fashioned social views.

WOMAN

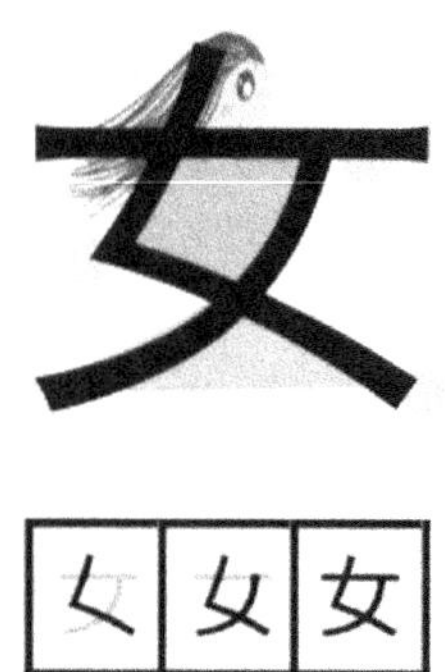

Try it:

CHILD 子

The radical for **"child"** (子) is a favorite among beginners. Not only is it easy to write, but it also functions as a very common **stand-alone *kanji*** meaning "child" or "offspring".

This radical, also known as こ (ko), is a clear pictogram of a baby. In its most ancient form, the character 子 depicted a large head, emphasizing the proportions of an infant, a horizontal stroke to represent the baby's arms reaching out, and a curved vertical stroke to represent the legs wrapped together in clothes or a blanket. Over time, these features were simplified into the three-stroke character we use today.

Beyond just "children," this radical often implies **growth**, **nurturing**, or **smallness**. **Common examples of the radical 子:**

- 好 (すき – to like): This combines **woman** (女) and **child** (子). A woman with her child is a classic image of "goodness" or something that is "liked."

- 学 (まなぶ – to study/learn): This shows a **child** (子) under a roof, symbolizing a school or a place of growth.

- 孫 (まご – grandchild): This combines **child** (子) with the radical for **thread/lineage** (系), representing the continuation of the family line.

CHILD

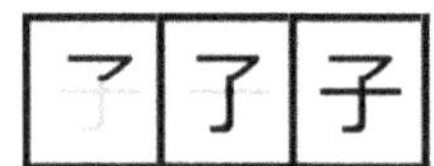

Try it:

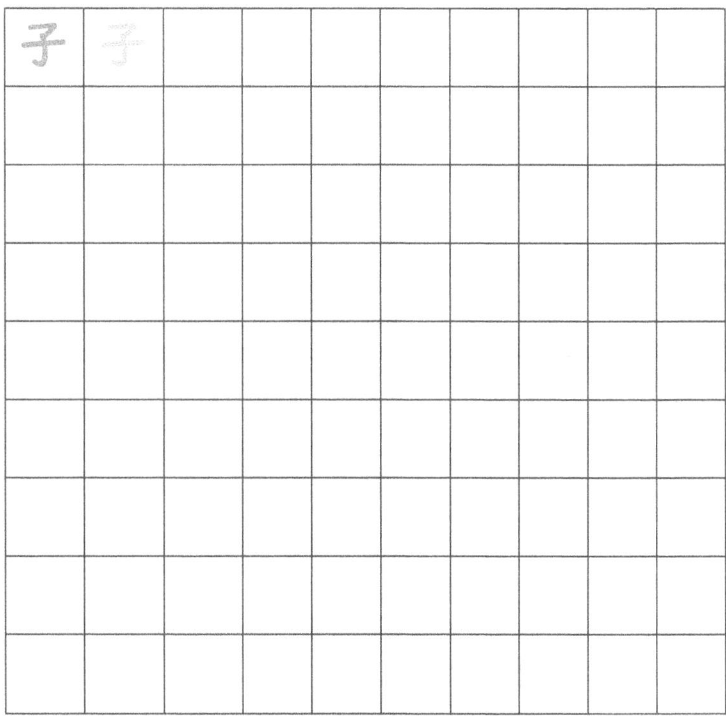

ROOF 宀

The radical for **"roof"** (宀) is a literal and intuitive component. It signifies a shelter, and it defines the space where ancient human life took place: the home.

Known in Japanese as うかんむり (*ukanmuri*), this radical is a classic pictogram. The top dot represents the **ridge** of a roof, while the horizontal line and the downward-curving strokes represent the **eaves and walls**.

When 宀 appears, it almost always points to one of two themes:

1. **Living Spaces and Buildings:** Direct references to physical structures or rooms.

   - 宅 (たく – home/residence)

   - 家 (いえ – house/family)

2. **Peace and Stability:** Because a roof provides shelter from the surroundings, it evolved to represent safety and protection.

   - 安 (やすい – cheap/peaceful): This shows a **woman** (女) safe under a **roof** (宀). In ancient times, a woman at home was a symbol of peace and security.

   - 定 (さだめる – to establish/fix): Suggests something settled firmly under a roof.

ROOF

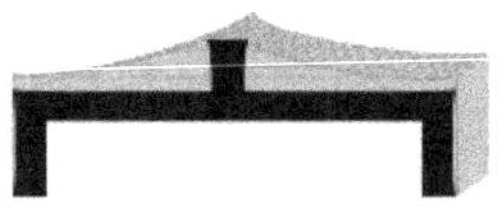

Try it:

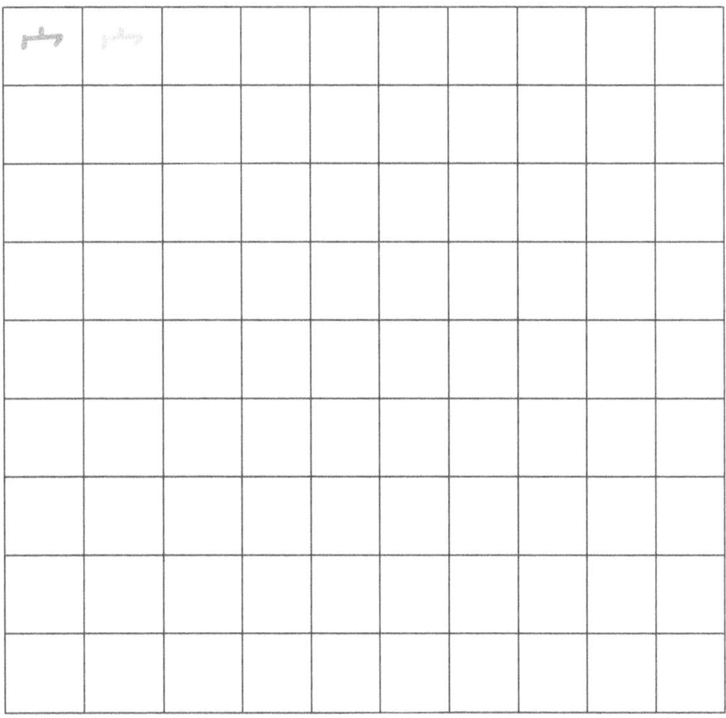

MEASUREMENT 寸

The radical "**measurement**" (寸) is a fascinating component that combines the concepts of physical measurement with human action. While it acts as a stand-alone *kanji* representing a traditional unit of length, its role as a radical is much broader.

Known in Japanese as **すん** (*sun*), this character has a very specific anatomical origin. It was originally a combination of a **hand** (又) and a **single horizontal mark** (一). The mark indicates the **pulse point** on the wrist. Because this distance was roughly consistent on every adult, it became a standard unit of measurement—approximately **3.03 cm** (known as one *sun*).

Since it represents both a "measurement" and a "hand" it usually brings one of two meanings to a *kanji*:

1. **Rules, Law, and Regulation:** Since it is a standard unit of measure, it symbolizes sticking to a "rule."

   - 将 (しょう – commander/leader): Someone who upholds the rules and leads the hand.

2. **Hand Actions and Guidance:** It represents the hand performing a precise or controlled movement.

   - 導 (みちびく – to guide): To lead someone by the hand along a path.

   - 専 (せん – exclusive/specialty): Originally represented a hand turning a spindle, implying focused manual work.

MEASUREMENT

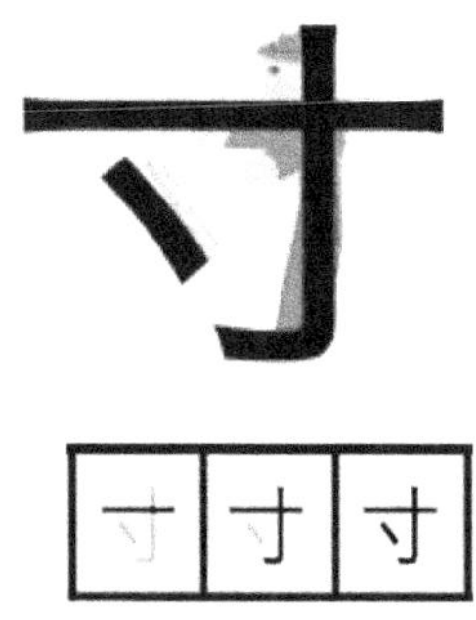

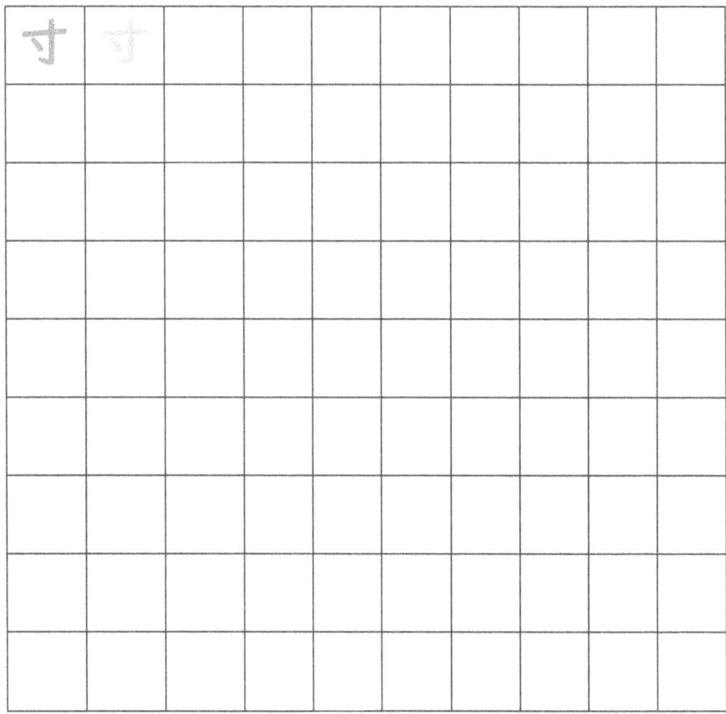

Try it:

SMALL 小

Just as there is a radical for "big," there is a corresponding radical for **"small"** (小). This radical is an essential for describing size, but it also carries deep cultural connotations regarding status, degree, and humility.

Known in Japanese as しょう (*shou*), this character is one of the most straightforward pictograms. The earliest forms of 小 consisted of **three small dots**, resembling tiny grains of sand or pebbles. Over time, the center dot was elongated into a vertical hooked stroke, and the two side dots became the slanted strokes we see today.

When you encounter 小 as a radical, it typically points to a volume or area:

- 少 (すこし – few/a little): This is the "small" radical with one extra stroke, literally meaning "a small amount."

- 尖 (とがる – to taper): This places **small** (小) on top of **big** (大). Something that goes from big to small is, by definition, tapered or pointed!

When the "small" radical appears at the **top** of a *kanji*, the two side dots often point **inward** or look like three vertical flicks (⺌). This is called しょうかんむり (*shoukanmuri*). You can see this in:

- 尚 (しょう – esteem)

- 当 (あたる – to hit/target)

SMALL

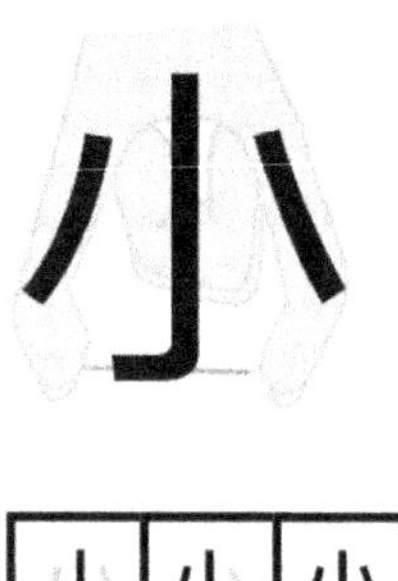

Try it:

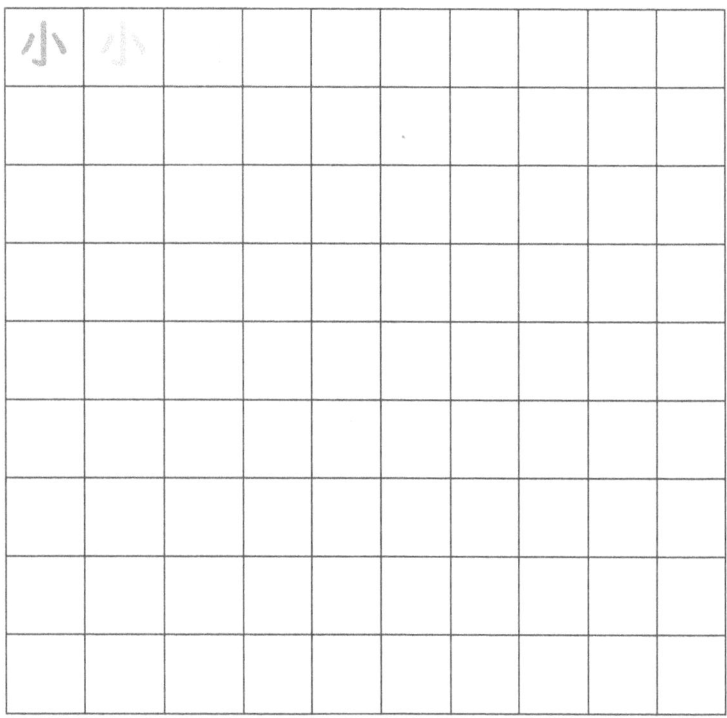

CORPSE 尸

The radical for **"corpse"** (尸) is a fascinating and complex component. Known in Japanese as **しかばね** (*shikabane*), it actually possesses three distinct identities inherited from ancient scripts. To understand this radical, you have to look at what is "hiding" underneath it.

While it looks like a simple "flag," the ancient origins tell three very different stories.

1. **The Reclining Person:** In ancient ancestral rites, a living person (often a grandson) would wear the clothes of the deceased and sit still to "house" the spirit of the ancestor and receive offerings.

    *   屍 (しかばね – corpse): The most literal use, combining the "body" (尸)with "death" (死).

2. **The Dwelling:** it is a simplified version of a building radical, representing a room, or a living space.

    *   居 (いる – to reside/be): A **shelter** (尸) where one sits for a "long time/old" (古).

3. **The Anatomy:** Finally, 尸 can represent the buttocks or the rear of the human body, particularly in relation to physiological functions.

    *   尿 (にょう – urine): Very literal—**water** (水) coming from the **body/rear** (尸).

CORPSE

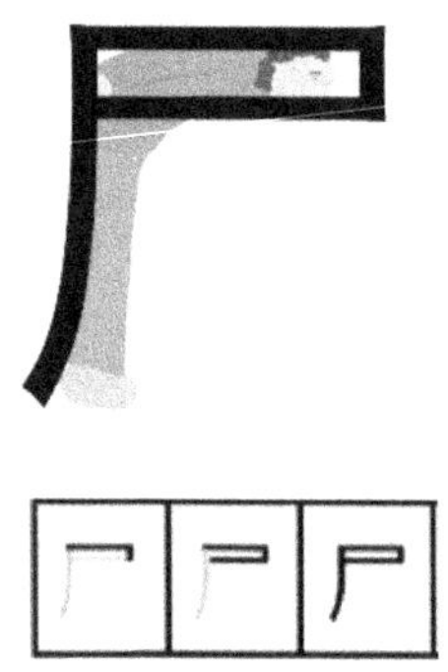

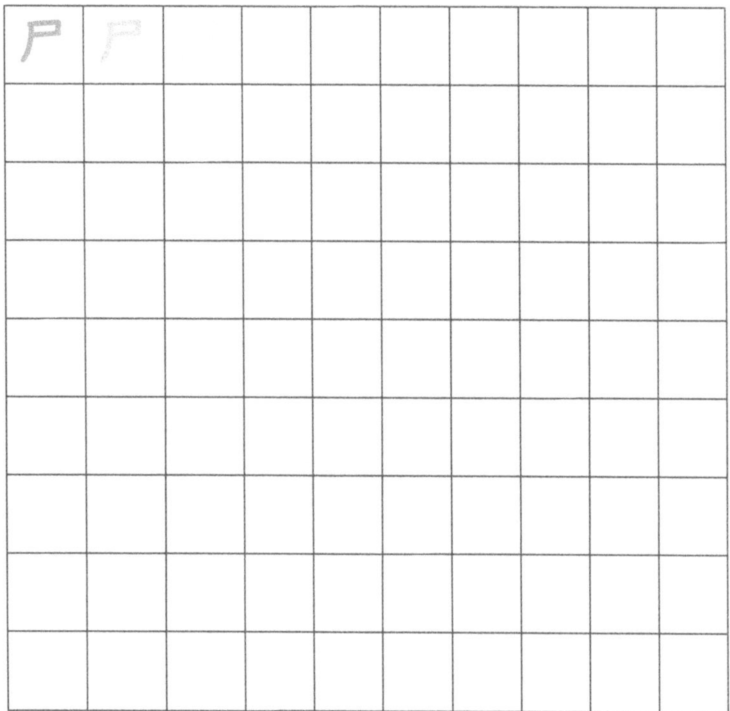

Try it:

ROAD 辶

The radical for **"road"** (辶), also known as しんにゅう (shinnyuu), is a fantastic example of a pictogram in action. It appears in over **100 *kanji***, making it one of the most useful components for a Japanese learner to recognize.

In its original, more complex form (辵), you can clearly see the two parts that created this radical:

- **The top (彳):** Represented a crossroad.

- **The bottom (止):** Represented a human foot.

Combined, they created the meaning of **"a foot walking along a road."** Over centuries, this was simplified into the fluid, wave-like shape we use today: 辶.

When you see 辶 wrapping around a character, the meaning relates to one of these three themes:

1. **Physical Movement:**

   - 追 (おう – to chase)

2. **Path and Space:**

   - 道 (みち – road/way)

3. **The Passage of Time:**

   - 速 (はやい – fast)

   - 週 (しゅう – week): Representing the "cycle" of time moving forward.

ROAD

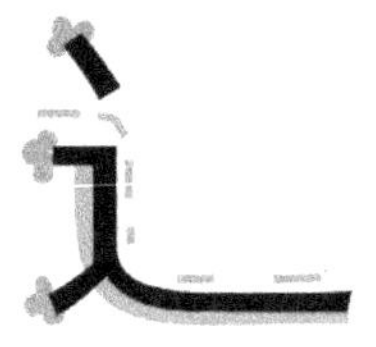

Try it:

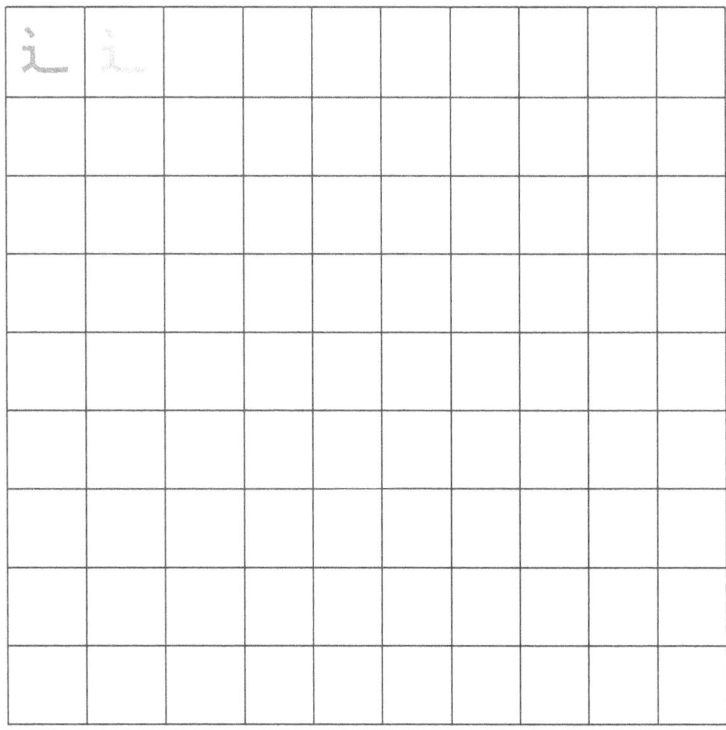

MOUNTAIN 山

The radical for **"mountain"** (山) is a foundational component that beginners often recognize immediately. Because it functions as both a common stand-alone *kanji* (やま - *yama*) and a radical, it serves as a reliable anchor for learning more complex characters.

 This character is a classic pictogram that vividly outlines the contour of a mountain range. Originally, it depicted **three mountain peaks**. The center stroke is the highest, representing the main summit, while the two shorter strokes on either side represent the surrounding peaks, all connected by a single baseline representing the earth.

When 山 is used as a radical, it typically classifies *kanji* into two main scenarios:

1. **Geography and Mountain Activities:**

   - 岩 (いわ – rock/boulder): Depicts a "mountain" (山) made of "stone" (石).

   - 峠 (とうげ – mountain pass/crisis): Combines "mountain" (山) with "up" (上) and "down" (下). It is the literal point where you stop going up and start going down!

2. **Mountain-like Shapes:**

   - 岡 (おか – hill/mound): Represents a smaller, rounded elevation.

MOUNTAIN

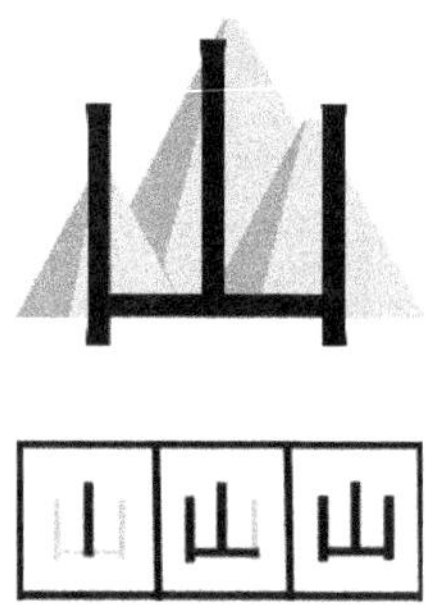

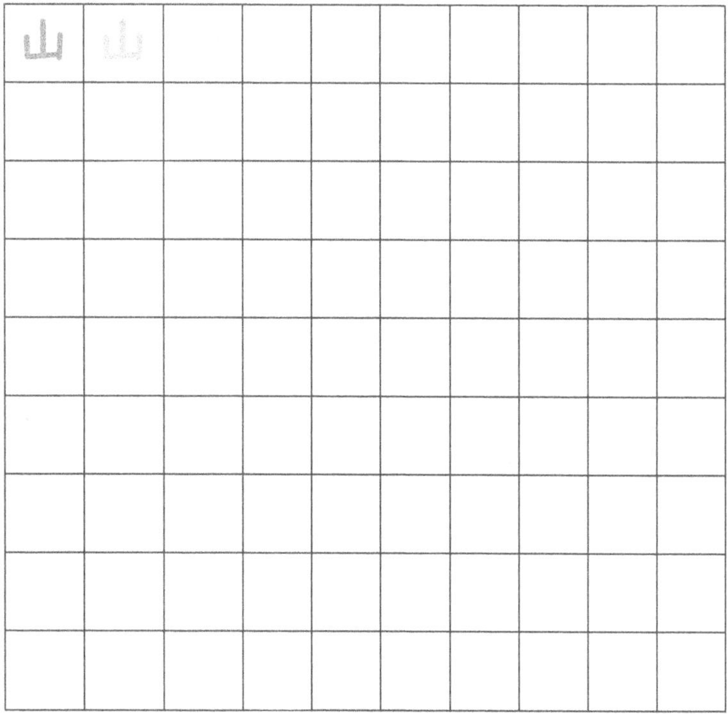

Try it:

CRAFT 工

The radical for **"craft"** or **"construction"** (工) is a simple but powerful symbol. Whether it acts as a stand-alone *kanji* or as a component in a larger character, it brings the energy of building, tools, and human skill.

工 Known in Japanese as たくみ (Takumi), this radical has two main historical interpretations:

1. It is often seen as a **carpenter's right-angle ruler**, used to ensure precision in manufacturing and architecture.

2. Another belief is that it represents an ancient **construction tool** used for ramming and compacting earth to create solid foundations.

When 工 appears as a radical, it typically signifies:

1. **Architecture, tools, or Skill:**

    *   左 (ひだり – Left): This is the combination of **hand** (ナ) and **tool** (工). Historically, the left hand was the one used to hold the tool while working.

    *   巧 (たくみ – Skilled): Directly uses the "craft" radical to describe someone who has mastered a technical ability.

    *   差 (さ – Difference/Distinction): Originally related to "measuring" work, which eventually led to the modern meaning of "discrepancy."

CRAFT

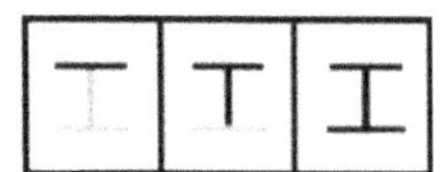

Try it:

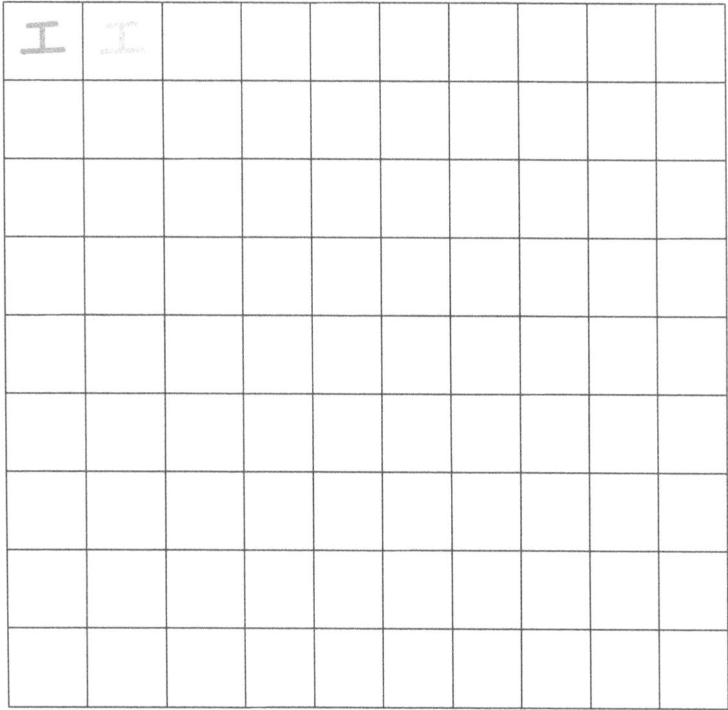

CLOTH 巾

The radical for **"cloth"** (巾) is a significant component that records the history of ancient textiles. It represents more than just a piece of fabric; it tracks the development of human clothing and the transition from animal skins to woven materials.

Known in Japanese as **はば** (*haba*), this radical is a pictogram of a **hanging cloth**: It depicts a piece of fabric draped over a horizontal bar or hanging from a hook. In its earliest forms, you could see the folds of the fabric. Today, it has been simplified into three clean strokes, but the image of something "hanging" remains.

When 巾 appears in a *kanji*, it typically refers to a single piece of cloth, and it usually falls into these three categories:

1. **Fabric:**

   - 布 (ぬの – linen/cloth)

   - 帆 (ほ – sail): a cloth that catches the wind

2. **Clothing and Accessories:**

   - 帯 (おび – sash/belt): An important accessory in a kimono.

3. **Functional Drapes:**

   - 帳 (ちょう – curtain/notebook): Originally a cloth curtain used to partition a room.

CLOTH

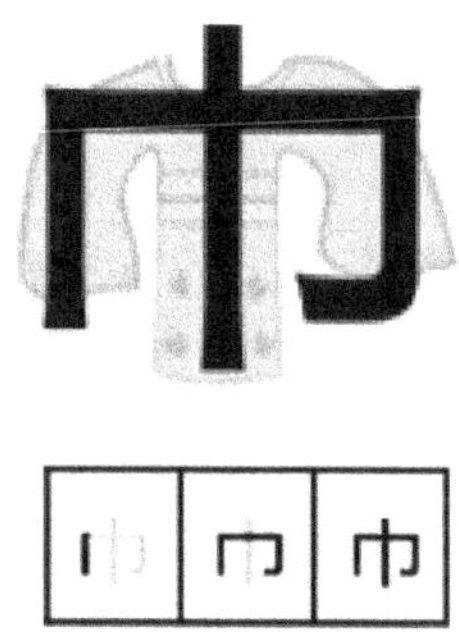

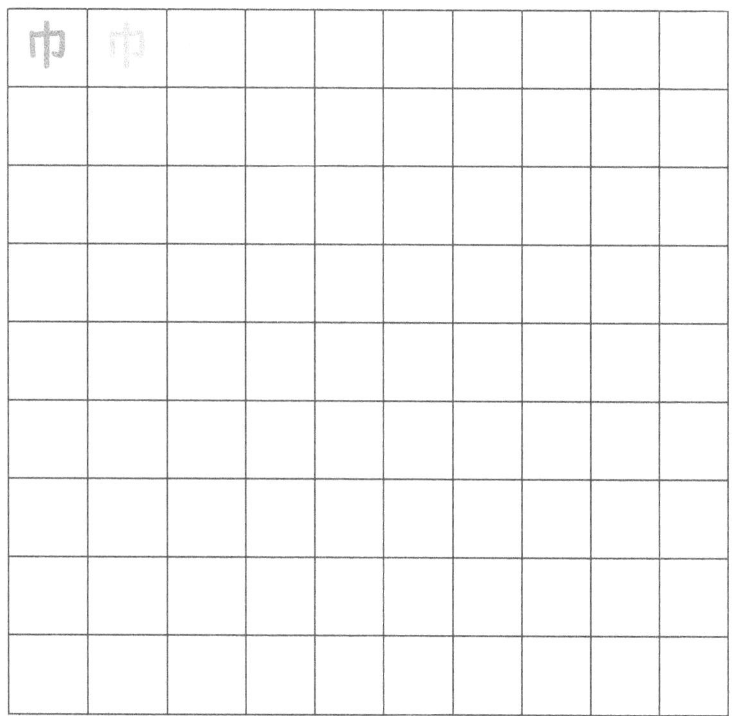

Try it:

BUILDING 广

The radical for **"Building"** (广) is a vital component in Japanese, used to describe architecture, man-made spaces, and the concept of residence. It bridges the gap between natural landscapes and human construction.

Known in Japanese as **まだれ** (*madare*), this radical is a pictogram of a simple dwelling. Unlike a freestanding house, this specifically represents a structure built against a mountain cliff for extra support:

The top dot represents the ridge or chimney of the roof.
The slanted stroke represents the slope of the roof.
The vertical line represents the supporting walls.

When 广 appears, it usually categorizes the *kanji* into one of three areas:

1. **Buildings:** Government offices, shops, or warehouses.

    - 庁 (ちょう – government office)

2. **Nature and the Description of Space:** Concepts involving size or designated areas.

    - 広 (ひろい – wide/spacious)

3. **Residence and Furniture:** Items or actions related to staying inside.

    - 床 (とこ – bed / ゆか – floor)

BUILDING

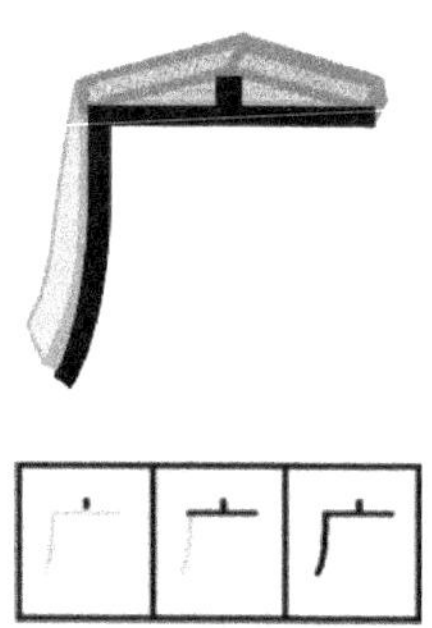

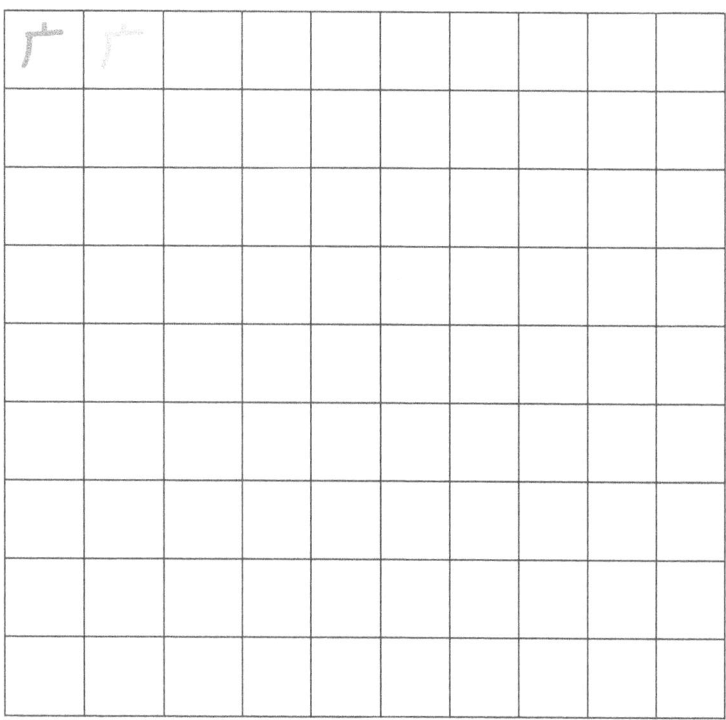

Try it:

BOW 弓

The radical for **"bow"** (弓) is a visually striking pictogram that appears in many characters related to archery, tension, and physical strength.

Known in Japanese as **ゆみ** (*yumi*), this radical is a literal drawing of a **strung bow**: You can see the handgrip in the center, and the string attachment points at both ends. Because a bow is designed to be bent and released, this radical often carries the abstract meaning of **tension**, **springiness**, and **extension**.

When 弓 is used as a radical, the *kanji* usually falls into one of these four categories:

1. **Archery:**

   - 弦 (つる – bowstring)

2. **Actions of Tension:**

   - 引 (ひく – to pull/draw): A visual of a line being pulled back by a bow.

3. **Strength and Form:**

   - 強 (つよい – strong): Represents a bow with a high degree of tension.

4. **Expansion and Space:**

   - 弘 (ひろい – broad/vast): The idea of a bow being drawn wide to cover a large distance.

BOW

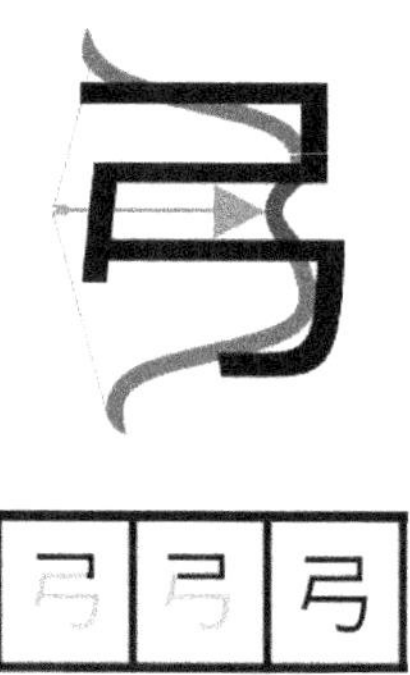

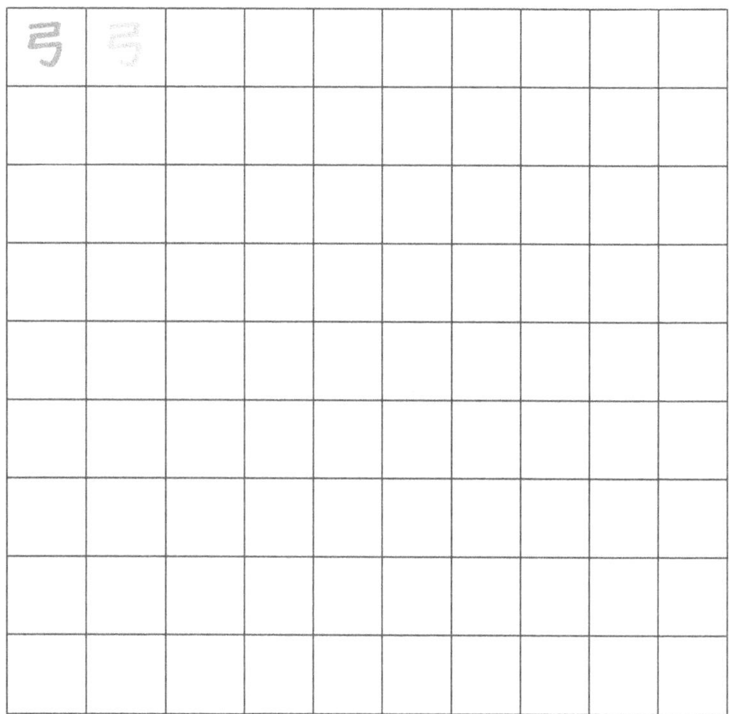

Try it:

HAIR 彡

The radical for **"hair"** or **"ornament"** (彡) is one of the most aesthetically pleasing components in Japanese. It represents the "texture" of the world—whether that is the literal hair on an animal or the abstract "pattern" of an object's surface.

Known in Japanese as さんづくり (*sandukuri*), this radical is a pictogram consisting of three long, sweeping strokes. Originally, this radical mimicked animal hair, or the texture of an object's surface. In the logic of *kanji*, these three strokes represent **luster**, **decoration**, or the **outward appearance** that makes something beautiful.

Though it appears in a relatively small number of *kanji*, the meanings are quite specific:

1. **Patterns, Forms, and Colors:**

    - 形 (かたち – shape/form): The outward "pattern" of a thing.

    - 影 (かげ – shadow/image): The "pattern" cast by the sun (日).

2. **Hair and Personal Appearance:**

    - 彦 (ひこ – an ancient title for an accomplished man): Often used in names, it implies a man who is "polished" or "ornamented" with talent.

HAIR

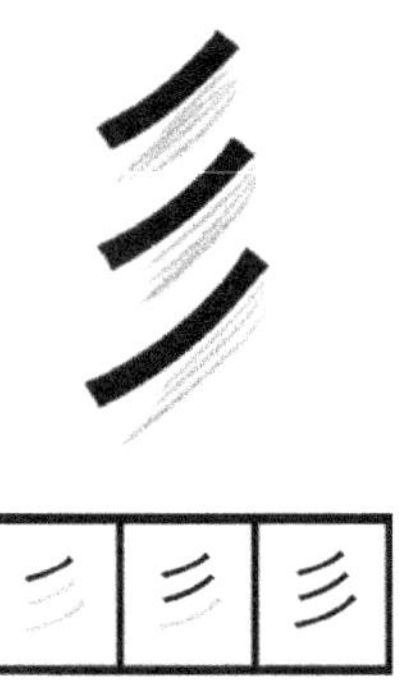

Try it:

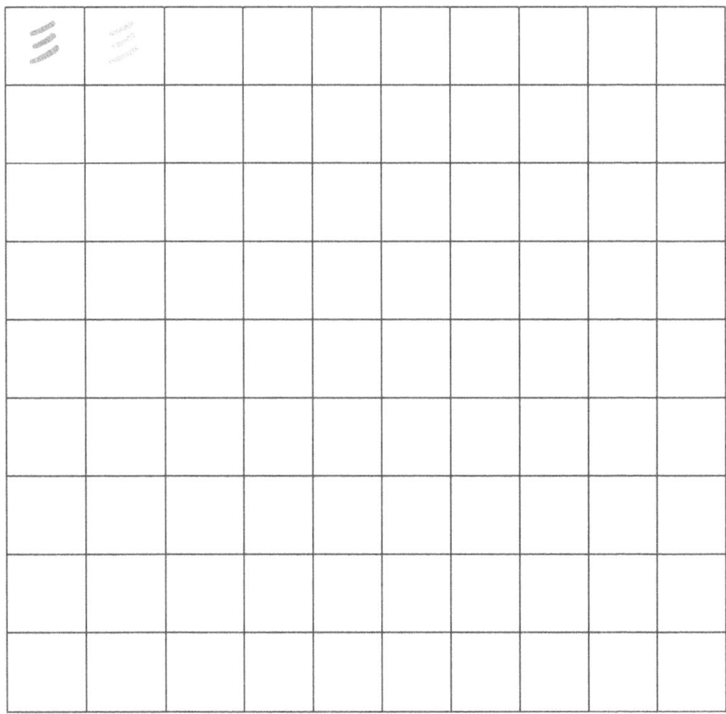

GOING 彳

The radical for **"going"** (彳) is a staple of the Japanese language. It is a common component that helps define how we move through space and interact with others.

Known in Japanese as **ぎょうにんべん** (*gyouninben*), this radical is a pictogram with a clever origin. To understand 彳, you have to look at the full *kanji* for **"go"** (行). In its ancient form, 行 was a picture of a **crossroad**. The radical 彳 is literally the **left-hand side** of that crossroad, representing the act of stepping out onto the path.

When you see 彳 as a radical, it typically falls into one of three categories:

1. **Movement and the Act of Walking:**

   - 往 (おう – depart/go): Representing movement along a path.

2. **Roads and Spatial Concepts:**

   - 後 (あと – behind/after): Originally depicted a person whose "steps" were being slowed down by a rope.

3. **Social Behavior and Conduct:**

   - 従 (したがう – to follow/obey): Depicts one person walking behind another on the road.

   - 徳 (とく – virtue/benevolence): Relates to "walking" the correct path of the heart.

GOING

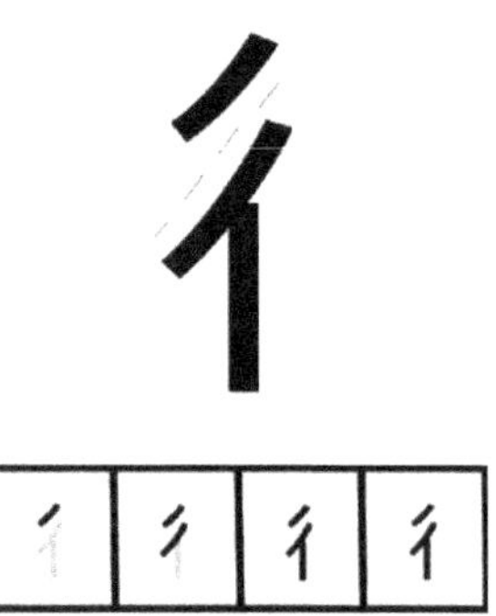

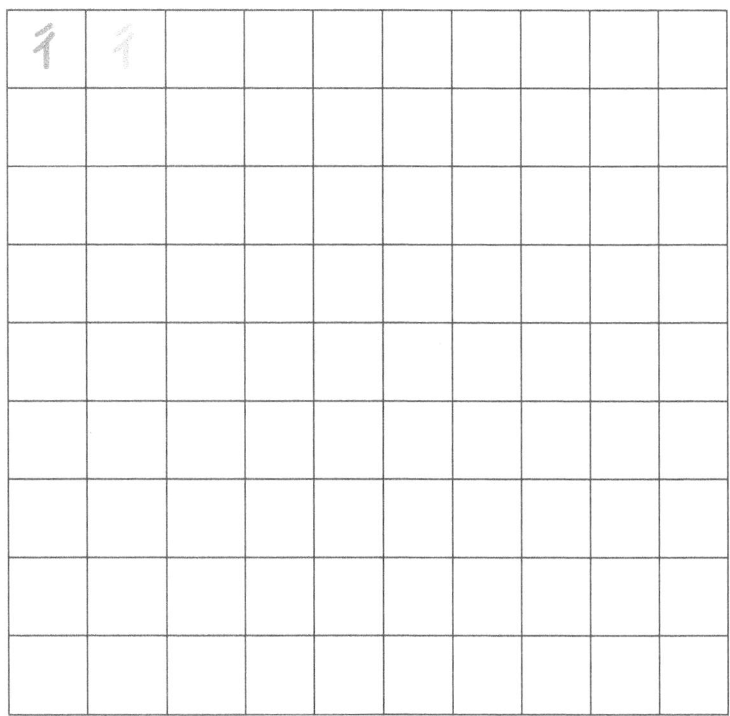

Try it:

SMALL THREAD 幺

The radical for **"short thread"** (幺) is a delicate but important component. It represents the very beginning of a thread—something thin, fragile, and immature. In the hierarchy of *kanji*, this radical almost always signifies things that are small, weak, or hidden.

 Known in Japanese as **いとがしら** (*itogashira*), which literally means **"thread head,"** this radical is a pictogram of a single twist of silk or rope.

You might notice that 幺 looks like the top half of the "thread" radical (糸). Because it is only "half" of a full thread, it represents something that is not yet fully formed or something exceptionally minute.

When 幺 appears as a radical, it usually guides the *kanji* into one of these three themes:

1. **Immaturity and Youth:**

    - 幼 (おさない – young/infant): Combines "small thread" (幺) with "strength" (力). It represents a child who has very little physical power.

2. **Hidden or Deep Concepts:**

    - 幽 (ゆう – faint/secluded): Suggests something hidden deep in the mountains.

3. **Extensions related to silk threads:**

    - 幾 (いく – how many/some): Originally referred to the fine order of threads on a loom.

SMALL THREAD

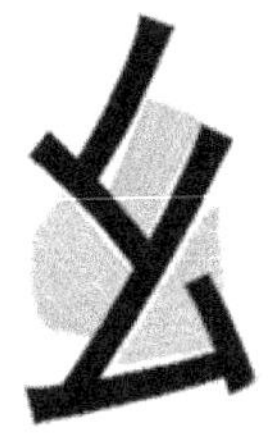

Try it:

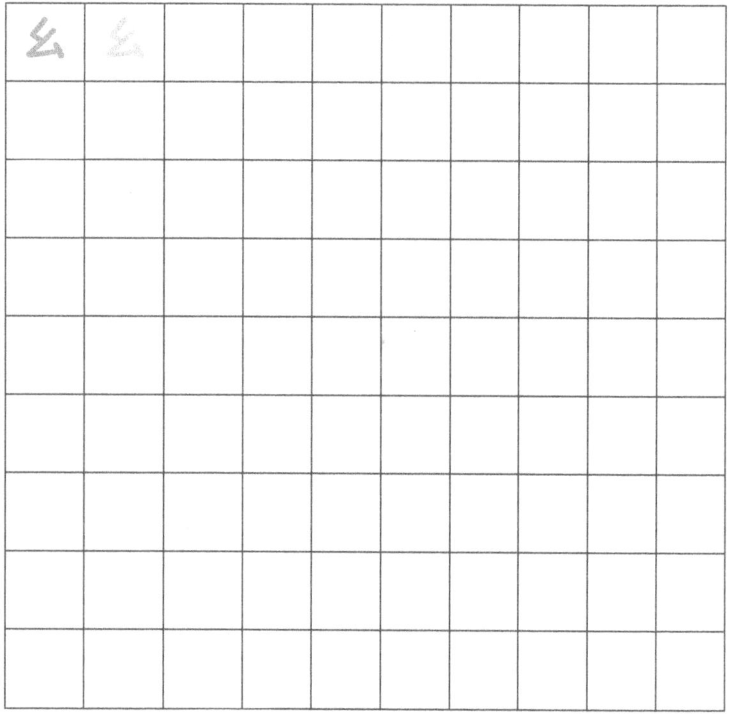

HEART 心 忄

The radical for **"heart"** (心 / 忄) is one of the most expressive components. While the stand-alone *kanji* for heart is 心, it transforms into a sleek, vertical shape when it appears on the left side of a character 忄.

In its most ancient forms, this radical was a literal pictogram of the **human heart,** with the dot in the middle representing the chambers and valves of the heart.

The form 忄, known in Japanese as りっしんべん (*risshinben*). The name literally means **"standing heart on the side."** It was compressed into three strokes, but its meaning remains rooted in the core of human feeling.

When you see 忄, or 心, the character's meaning can fall into three main categories:

1. **Emotions and Feelings:**

   - 怖 (こわい – scary/afraid): The heart feeling a "pressured" or "bound" state.

2. **Personality and States of Being:**

   - 快 (かい – pleasant/cheerful): A "bright" or "cleared" heart.

3. **Cognition and Memory:**

   - 忘 (わすれる – to forget): Your **heart** (心) is **lost/perished** (亡) regarding a certain thought.

HEART

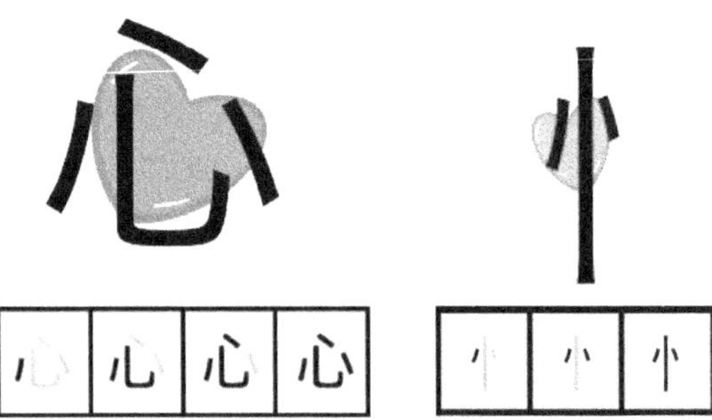

Try it:

HALBERD 戈

The radical for **"halberd"** (戈) is a striking representation of ancient weaponry culture. Beyond its literal meaning as a tool of war, it carries a deep cultural significance.

Known in Japanese as **ほこ** (*hoko*), this radical is a pictogram of a specific type of weapon. The 戈 consisted of a **long handle** with a **flat blade** mounted horizontally. This "T-shaped" design allowed soldiers on the ground to hook enemies off their chariots or strike at their heads.

When 戈 appears as a radical, it usually points toward one of these three categories:

1. **War, Conflict, and Violence:**

   - 戦 (*たたかう* – war/battle): Combines a "hunting tool" with the "halberd."

2. **Law, Discipline, and Protection:**

   - 戒 (*いましめる* – commandment): Depicts **two hands** (廾) holding a **halberd** (戈), symbolizing the act of guarding against a threat.

3. **Status and Identity:**

   - 成 (*なる* – to become/succeed): Historically related to reaching a stage where one can carry a weapon, symbolizing achievement.

HALBERD

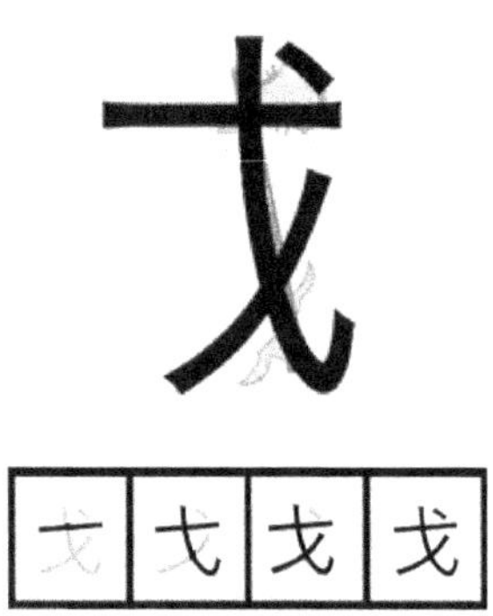

Try it:

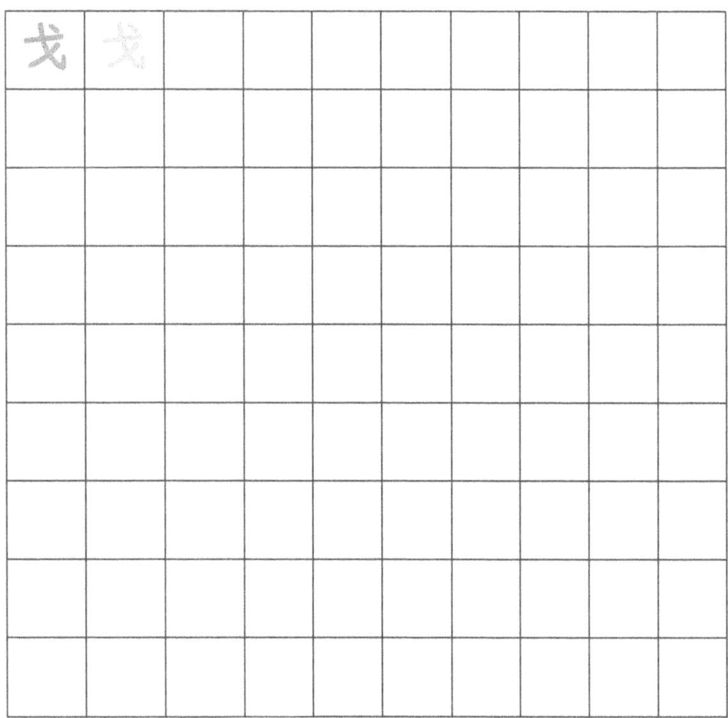

DOOR 戸

The radical for **"door"** (戸) is a significant pictogram that provides a window into ancient architecture and social organization. Its unique shape tells a specific story of how spaces were enclosed.

Known in Japanese as とだれ (*todare*), this radical is a literal drawing of a door. Unlike the radical for "Gate" (門), which represents a large, double-leaf entrance, 戸 represents a **single-leaf door**. You can see the top horizontal bar (the frame) and the vertical side representing the door itself swinging on its hinge. Historically, this refers to the entrance to a private room or a smaller residence, as opposed to the gates of a city.

As this radical evolved, its meaning expanded as follows:

1. **Architectural Components:**

   - 扉 (とびら – door): The literal word for a swinging door.

2. **Household and Domestic Life:**

   - 扇 (おうぎ – folding fan): It combines "door" (戸) and "feathers" (羽), describing a fan that opens and closes with a swinging motion.

   - 戻 (もどる – to return): Historically depicted a **dog** (犬) coming back through the **door** (戸). The modern commonly used character is a simplified form.

DOOR

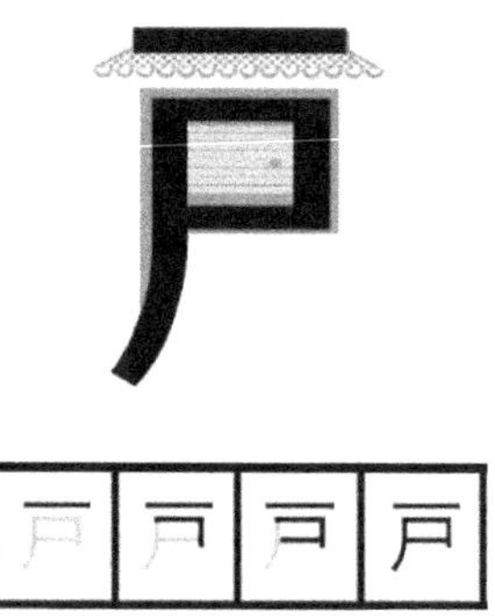

Try it:

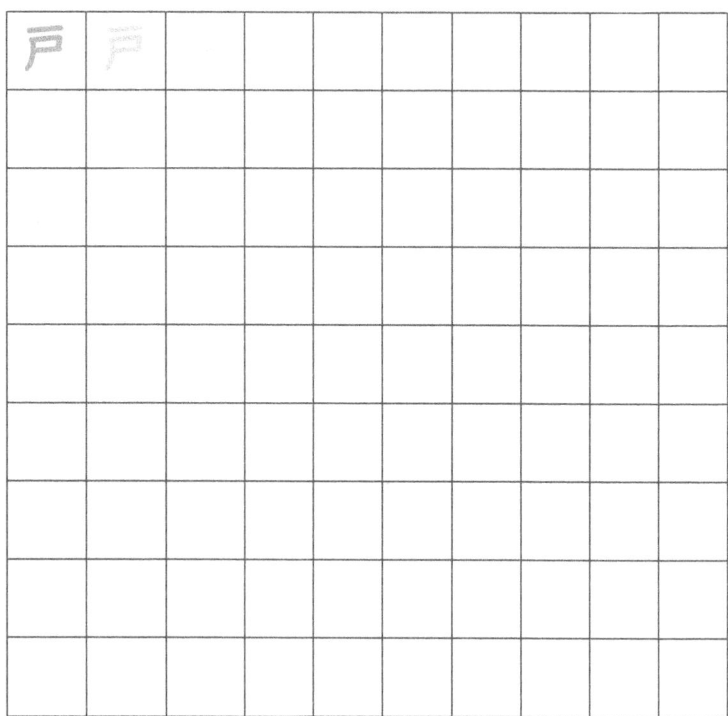

HAND 手 扌

The radical for **"hand"** (手 / 扌) is a cornerstone of the Japanese writing system. It doesn't just represent an organ for labor; it captures the essence of survival skills, and our ability to manipulate the world around us.

Known in its stand-alone form as て (*te*) and its side-variant as てへん (*tehen*), this radical is a clear pictogram of a human hand. In ancient scripts, you can vividly see five fingers at the top, connecting to a line representing the palm and the wrist at the bottom. When the hand moves to the left side of a character, it is compressed into 扌.

Because the hand is our primary tool, characters with this radical almost always involve a physical or metaphorical "touch."

1. **Physical Movements and Actions:**

   - 打 (うつ – to hit): A **hand** (扌) hitting a **nail**.

2. **Productive Labor and Skills:**

   - 技 (わざ – skill/technique): The dexterity of the **hand** (扌) used in a specific "branch" or field.

3. **Social Behavior and Power:**

   - 援 (えん – help/assist): The act of reaching out a **hand** (扌) to pull someone up.

   - 招 (まねく – to invite/beckon): Using a hand (扌) to call someone over.

HAND

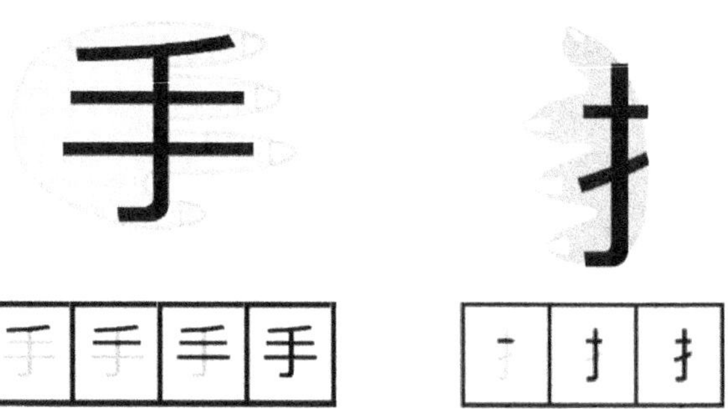

Try it:

STRIKE 攵

The radical for **"strike"** (攵) is a dynamic component. While it is often confused with the radical for "slowly" (夂), its origins are rooted in active influence and movement.

Known in Japanese as **ぼくづくり** (*bokudukuri*), this radical is a simplified version of the ancient character 攴, which depicts a **right hand** (the bottom strokes) holding a **stick or a whip** (the top strokes).

This radical doesn't just mean "to hit" in a violent sense. It represents the act of "prompting" someone to act, "guiding" a process, or "administering" a task.

When you see 攵 on the right side of a kanji, the meaning usually involves one of these three categories:

1. **Direct Force or Conflict:**

   - 敵 (て き – enemy): Originally referred to "striking" back at an equal opponent.

2. **Guidance and Education:**

   - 教 (お し え る – to teach): It depicts a child being guided to encourage learning.

   - 政 (せ い – government/politics)

3. **Order, Logic, and Reform:**

   - 数 (か ず – number): The act of tapping or "striking" items one by one to count them.

STRIKE

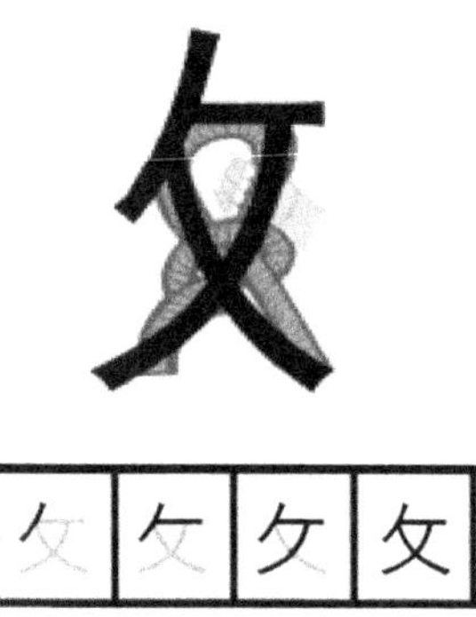

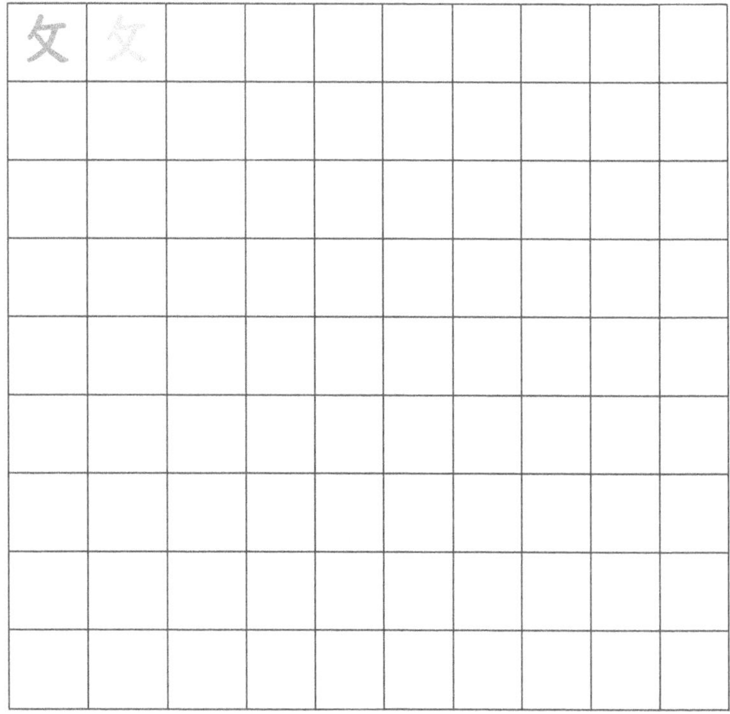

Try it:

DIRECTION 方

The radical for **"direction"** (方) is a unique character that serves as a cornerstone for geography and movement. While we primarily associate it with "way" or "side" today, its ancient roots tell a story of tools, boundaries, and parallel paths.

 Known in Japanese as **ほう** (*hou*), there are three major theories regarding its origin:

1. **The Hand-Plow:** The most widely accepted theory is that it depicts an ancient wooden plow. Here plowing defines **boundaries** and **direction**.

2. **Two Boats Side-by-Side:** Some paleographers believe it shows two boats lashed together.

3. **The Shackle:** A rarer theory suggests it represents a person in a wooden shackle.

When 方 appears as a radical, it usually falls into these two categories:

1. **Direction and Space:**

    *   方 (ほう – direction/way)

    *   於 (おいて – at/in/on): A grammatical particle used to indicate a location or "place" in space.

2. **Banners and Travel (The "Flag" Variant):**

    *   旅 (たび – travel): Originally depicted people gathered under a banner to go on a journey.

DIRECTION

方 方 方 方

Try it:

AXE 斤

The radical for **"axe"** (斤) is a clear window into the tools of ancient labor. Beyond just representing a weapon or a tool for chopping, it reflects the development of early industry, measurement, and construction.

Known in Japanese as **おの** (*ono*), this radical is a literal pictogram of a handheld axe. The top horizontal stroke represents the **blade**, while the vertical stroke represents the **wooden handle**.

In ancient times, the axe was the primary tool for clearing land and preparing timber for building, making it a symbol of progress and "breaking ground."

When 斤 appears as a radical, the *kanji* usually falls into one of these two categories:

1. **Cutting and Cleaving:**

    - 断 (だん – to cut off/disconnect): Shows the "axe" (斤) cutting through a thread or connection.

2. **Analysis and Construction:**

    - 新 (あたらしい – new): This character shows a **tree** (木), a **stand** (立), and an **axe** (斤). It represents the act of cutting fresh wood to build something brand new.

AXE

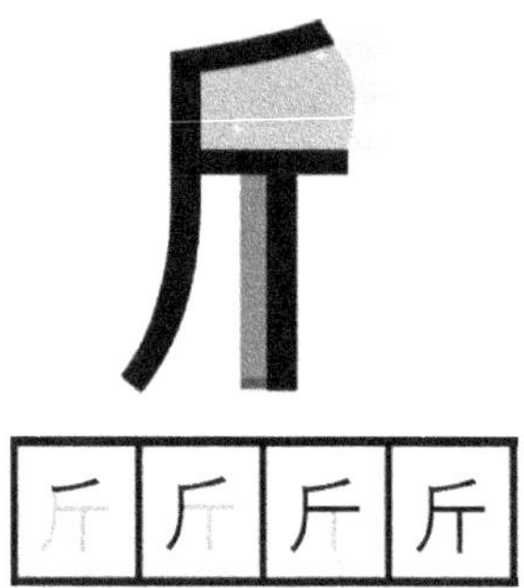

Try it:

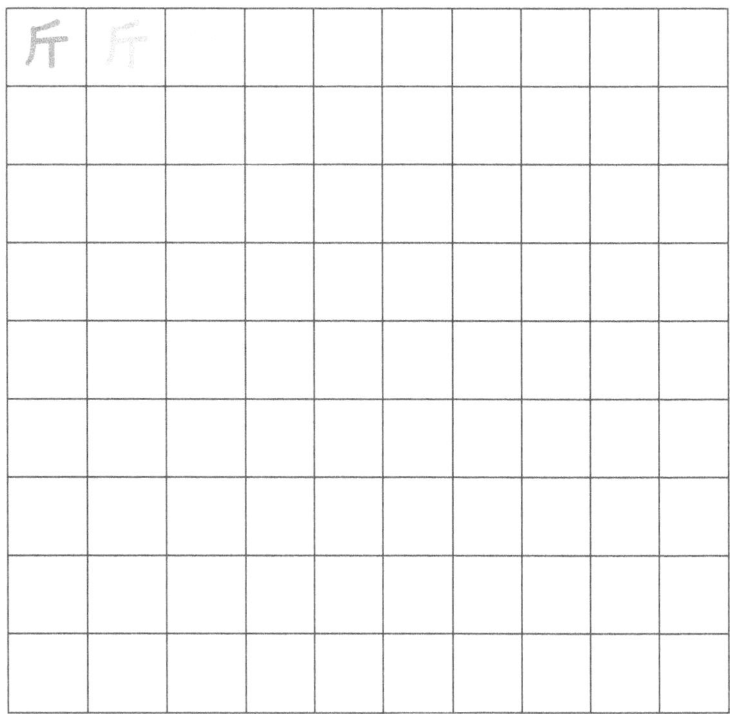

SUN 日

The radical for **"sun"** (日) is a cornerstone of Japanese writing. It serves as the primary indicator for anything related to the passage of time, the presence of light, or the cycles of nature.

Known in Japanese as ひ (*hi*), this is a classic pictogram. Originally a circle with a dot in the center. The outer square represents the sun's disk. The middle line was added not just to distinguish it from other characters, but to represent the **light** radiating from within. It signifies that this is a solid, glowing object, not an empty space.

When 日 acts as a radical, it almost always pulls the character into one of these three categories:

1. **Time and the Calendar:**

    - 旧 (きゅう – old/former): The sun (日) passing over a vertical line, representing time gone by.

2. **Light, Brightness, and Weather:**

    - 晴 (はれ– clear weather): The sun (日) bringing out the "blue" (青) of the sky.

    - 明 (あかるい– bright): The sun (日) and the moon (月), the two brightest objects in the sky.

3. **Position and Movement:**

    - 昇 (のぼる– to rise): The sun (日) moving upward.

SUN

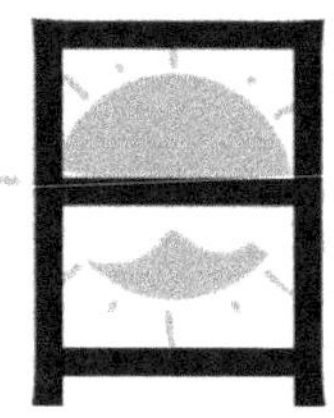

Try it:

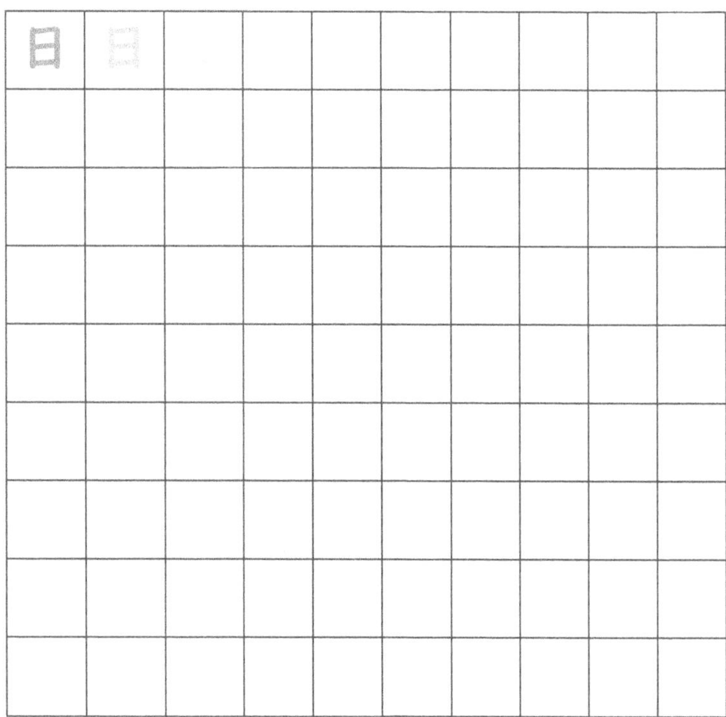

MOON 月

The radical for **"moon"** (月) is one of the most interesting and easily confused components in *kanji*. It is a "dual-purpose" radical with two completely different origins that merged into one shape over thousands of years.

 Known in Japanese as つき (*tsuki*), it represents two very different concepts depending on the character's meaning.

- **The "Celestial Moon" (月):** A pictogram of a crescent moon. In ancient times, the two horizontal lines inside represented the "dark" and "light" spots on the moon's surface. This version relates to **time, light, and the night**.

- **The "Meat" Radical (肉 / 月):** This was originally a pictogram of a **slice of meat** with ribs showing. Because it was difficult to write the complex "meat" shape (肉) inside other characters, it was simplified to look exactly like a moon (月). This version relates to **body parts and biology**.

When you see 月, you must check the context to see which "version" of the radical is at work:

1. **Time and Natural Cycles (Celestial Moon):**

   - 期 (き – period/term): A **moon** (月) cycle used to measure time against a "sieve/base" (其).

   - 朝 (あさ – morning): The **moon** (月) fading as the **sun** (日) rises through the **grass**.

MOON

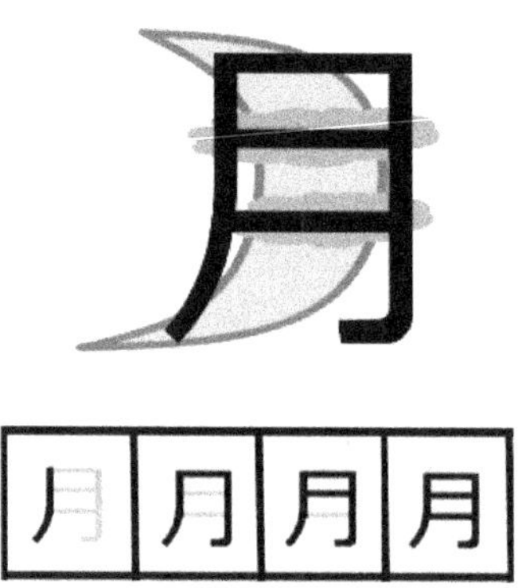

Try it:

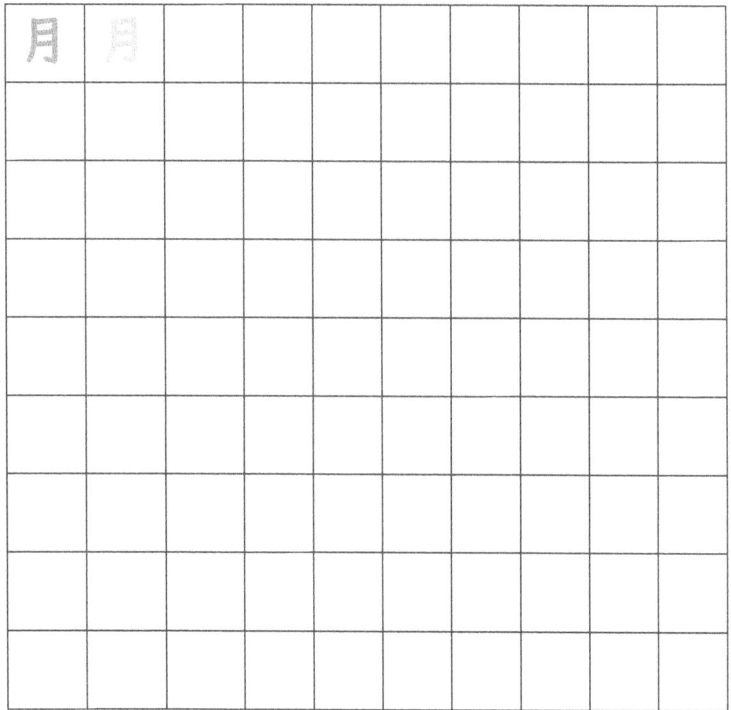

WOOD 木

The radical for **"wood"** or **"tree"** (木) is one of the most easily recognizable symbols in the Japanese language. It serves as the base of several characters, ranging from specific plant species to the everyday objects.

Known in Japanese as き (*ki*), this radical is a beautiful pictogram of a tree. The horizontal stroke and the top of the vertical line represent the branches. The vertical line represents the trunk. The two diagonal "legs" represent the roots anchoring the tree into the earth.

When 木 appears as a radical, it typically organizes *kanji* into these four functional categories:

1. **Parts of a Tree and Forest:**

   - 本 (もと – origin/book): A line added to the bottom to show the **base** or root.

2. **Specific Tree Types:**

   - 桜 (さくら – cherry blossom)

3. **Wooden Products and Tools:**

   - 机 (つくえ – desk)

4. **Abstract Properties and States:**

   - 朽 (くちる – to decay/rot): Describing the natural breakdown of wood over time.

WOOD

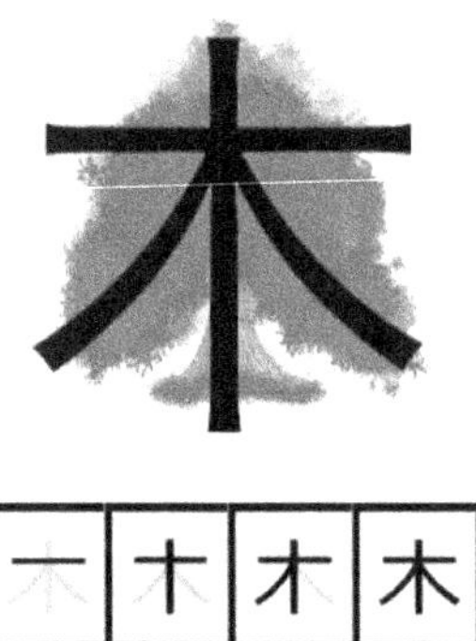

Try it:

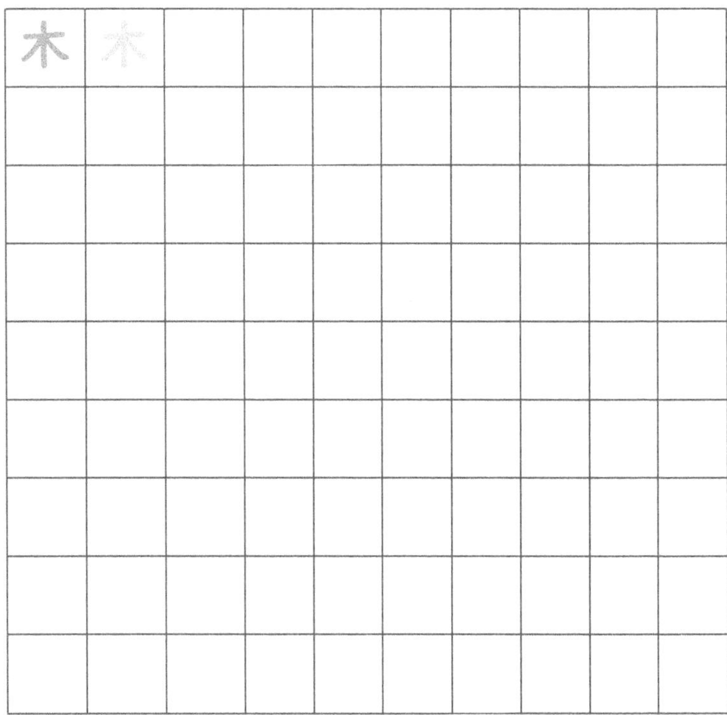

LACK 欠

The radical for **"lack"** or **"yawn"** (欠) is a fascinating pictogram that links physical actions of the mouth to the abstract feeling of insufficiency. It shows us that in the world of *kanji*, "wanting" something is often seen as having an "empty space" that needs to be filled with breath or substance.

Known in Japanese as **あくび** (*akubi*), this radical is a vivid drawing of a person in a specific state. It depicts a person with their **mouth wide open**. While it literally represents a **yawn**, it more broadly symbolizes **exhaling**, gasping for air, or the "gap" created when something is missing.

When 欠 appears in a character, it usually falls into one of these three categories:

1. **Breathing and Oral Actions:**

   - 歓 (かん – delight/joy): A person opening their mouth wide to cheer or shout with happiness.

2. **Lack and Insufficiency:**

   - 欠 (かく – lack/defect): The stand-alone character for something missing.

3. **Desire and Psychological States:**

   - 欲 (ほしい – want/desire): It represents a deep, cavernous craving.

LACK

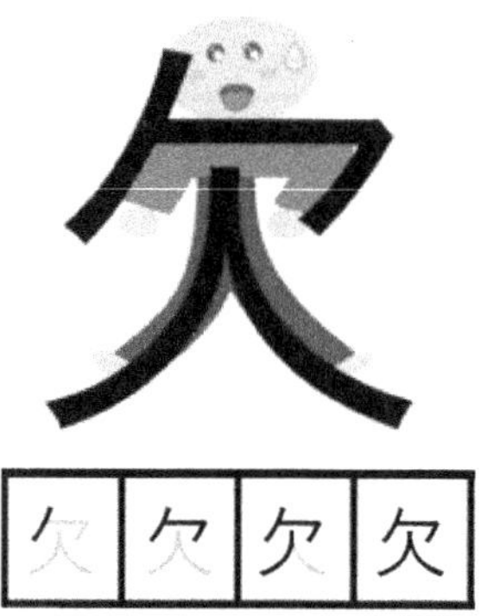

欠 欠 欠 欠

Try it:

STOP 止

The radical for **"stop"** (止) is a fascinating element that serves as the foundation for many characters related to movement, time, and even morality. While we know it today as "stop," its origin is rooted in the most basic form of human travel: the foot.

Known in Japanese as **とめる** (*tomeru*), this radical is a clear pictogram of a human foot. If you look at the ancient script, the top represents the **toes**, while the vertical and horizontal lines represent the **sole** and **heel**.

Initially, it simply meant "foot" or "to walk." However, just as a footprint marks the place where a step has finished, the meaning eventually shifted from the act of walking to the result of walking: **reaching a destination** and **stopping**.

When 止 appears in a character, it usually directs the meaning toward one of these two themes:

1. **Walking and Physical Movement:**

    *   歩 (あるく – to walk): Historically, this showed two feet (止), representing taking steps.

2. **Endpoints and Stoppage:**

    *   歳 (さい – year/age): This complex character includes 止 to represent the completion of a cycle—the "endpoint" of a year.

STOP

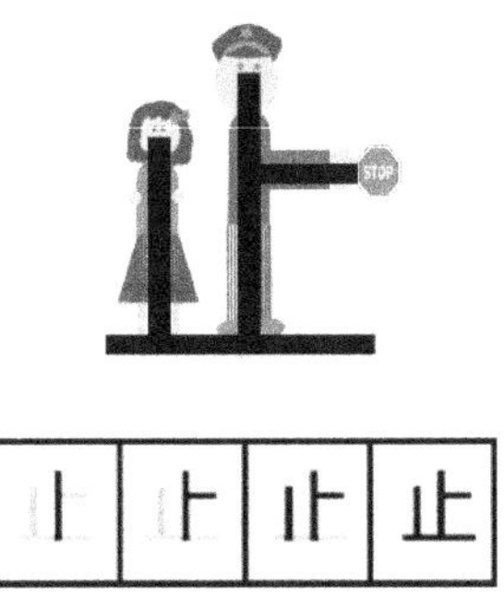

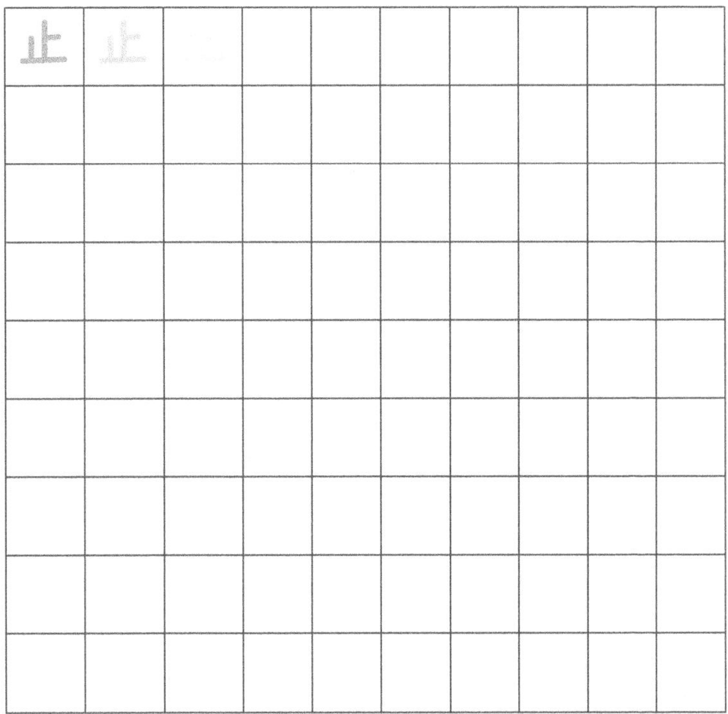

Try it:

DEATH 歹

The radical for **"death"** (歹) is a revealing component that captures ancient observations about the end of life. It is used in characters that deal with mortality, decay, and the remnants of what once was.

Known in Japanese as **がつへん** (*gatsuhen*), this radical is a grim but fascinating pictogram. In its earliest forms, it represented the **fragment of a skeleton**. It specifically depicts the state of bones after the flesh has decayed or been removed. Because it represents the "leftovers" of life, it naturally became the symbol for death, destruction, and anything that is "broken" beyond repair.

When 歹 appears on the left side of a *kanji*, it typically falls into one of these two categories:

1. **Literal Death and Mortality:**

    - 死 (し – death): The most famous example, showing a person next to a bone fragment (歹).

    - 殉 (じゅん – martyrdom): Following someone into death or sacrificing oneself.

2. **Decay and Remains:**

    - 残 (のこる – to remain/be left over): Originally related to the bones left over after a disaster or slaughter. Today, it is the standard word for "remnants."

DEATH

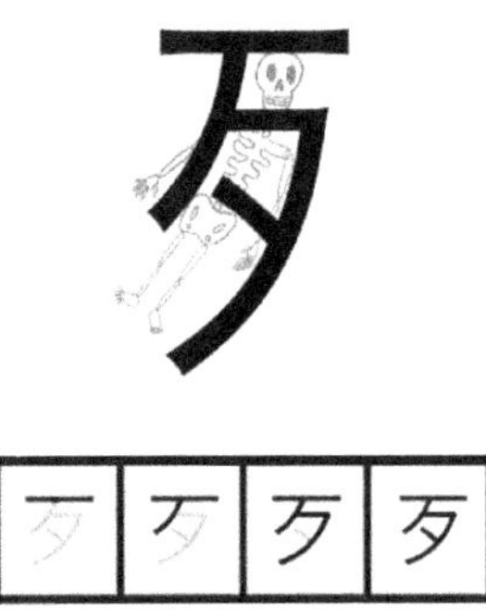

Try it:

WEAPON 殳

The radical for **"weapon"** (殳) is a heavy-duty component that represents physical force, impact, and the use of long-handled tools. While it is often called a "spear" or "halberd", it specifically represents a blunt, crushing weapon used to shatter armor or shields.

Known in Japanese as **るまた** (*rumata*), this radical is a pictogram of a powerful ancient weapon. The top part represents a **long wooden pole** with a heavy, blunt head (angular or round). The bottom part (又) is the common symbol for a **right hand** gripping the handle. Unlike a sword that cuts, the 殳 relied on its 12-foot length and weight to deliver a massive blow.

When 殳 appears on the right side of a character, it usually falls into these two categories:

1. **Striking and Attacking:**

   - 殺 (ころす – to kill): Shows a "weapon" (殳) being used against a target, signifying the end of life through force.

2. **Use of Tools and Labor:**

   - 殻 (から – shell/husk): This depicts the act of striking something to remove its hard outer covering.

   - 段 (だん – step/grade): Originally related to a "hammering" action used to create levels or stairs in a cliffside.

WEAPON

Try it:

WATER 水 氵

The radical for **"water"** (水) is a foundational element that vividly records the ancient relationship between humans and the natural world.

Known as (水) **みず** (*mizu*), and (氵) **さんすい** (*sansui*), this radical is a classic pictogram. The central stroke represents the **main stream**, while the four smaller strokes on the sides represent **droplets, or splashing water**.

To keep the *kanji* balanced and compact, the "Water" radical is simplified into **three dots** on the left 氵.

This radical typically flows into one of these four categories:

1. **Geography and Bodies of Water:**

   - 池 (いけ – pond): Water held in a specific place

2. **Physical Properties and States:**

   - 汽 (き – steam/vapor): Water becoming "breath-like" or gaseous.

3. **Human Actions and Behaviors:**

   - 泳 (およぐ – to swim)

4. **Abstract and Extended Meanings:**

   - 永 (えい – eternity): A depiction of a long, never-ending river system.

WATER

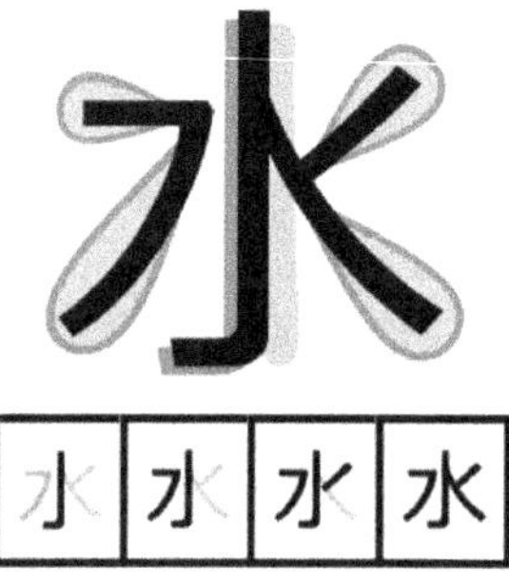 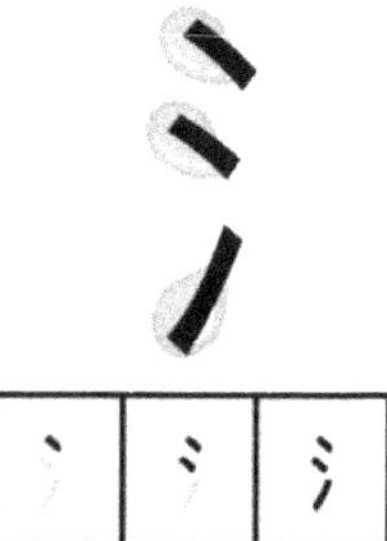

Try it:

COW 牛

The radical for **"cow"** or **"ox"** (牛) highlights the vital role these animals played in ancient society, not just as sources of food, but as essential tools for agriculture and the highest form of religious offering.

Known as うし (*ushi*), this radical is one of the most accurate pictograms in the *kanji* system, depicting an ox's head viewed from the front. The **top horizontal strokes** represent the large, upward-curving horns. The **vertical stroke** is the bridge of the nose/face. The **lower diagonal strokes** represent the ears.

When 牛 appears in a character, it generally signifies one of these three themes:

1. **Descriptions of Cattle:**

   - 牝 (めす – female): A **cow** (牛) and a "spoon" (匕, representing the female shape).

   - 牡 (おす – male): A **cow** (牛) and "soil" (土, representing the male role).

2. **Farming and Herding:**

   - 牧 (ぼく – breed): A **cow** (牛) being guided by a **hand with a stick** (攵)

3. **Sacrifice and Sacredness:**

   - 牲 (せい – sacrifice/offering): Life (生) and **cow** (牛).

COW

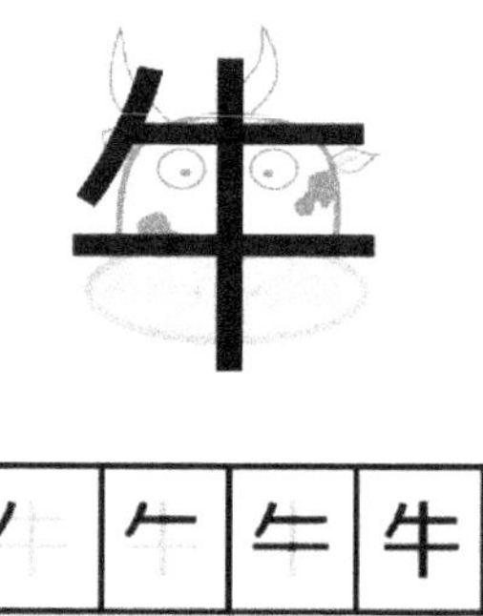

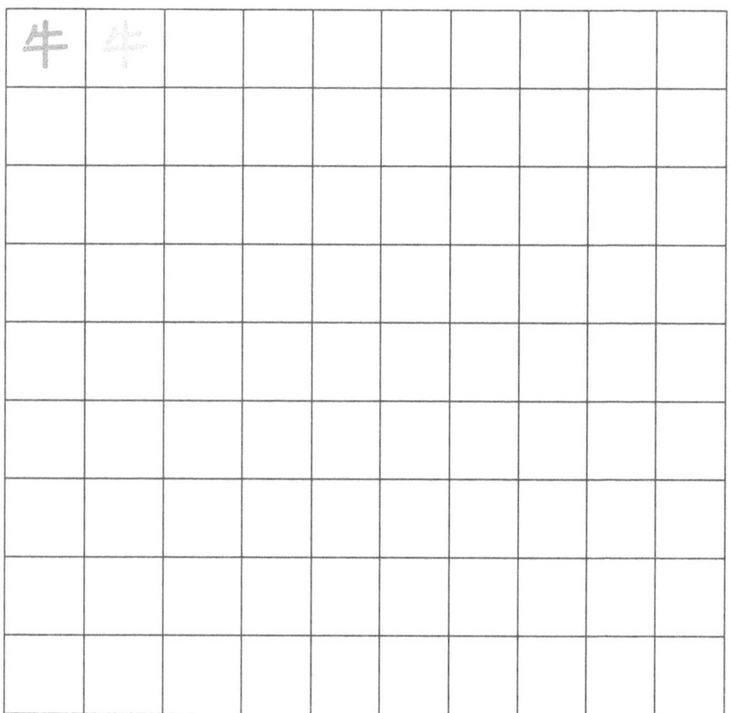

Try it:

DOG 犬 犭

The radical for **"dog"** or **"Beast"** (犬 / 犭) is a vivid reminder of humanity's ancient relationship with the animal kingdom. While it originally depicted a canine, it evolved to represent several wild animals, hunting, and even certain "unrestrained" human behaviors.

Known as **いぬ** (*inu*) when standing alone and **けものへん** (*kemonohen*) when on the left, this radical has a very literal origin. Originally the character was a **vertical pictogram of a dog**. You could see the head, the body standing sideways, and the **tail curling upward**. To save space, it was compressed into three strokes (犭) on the left side.

When you see 犭 , think of the "wild" or "animalistic" side of the world. It usually falls into these three categories:

1. **Animal Names:**

    *   猫 (ねこ – cat): This is a fun irony for students. The *kanji* for **cat** uses the **dog** radical!

2. **Hunting and the Wild:**

    *   狩 (かる – to hunt)

3. **Character and Behavior:** Describing human traits through animal metaphors.

    *   狂 (くるう – insane): A "beast-like" (犭) state of mind where one loses human reason.

DOG

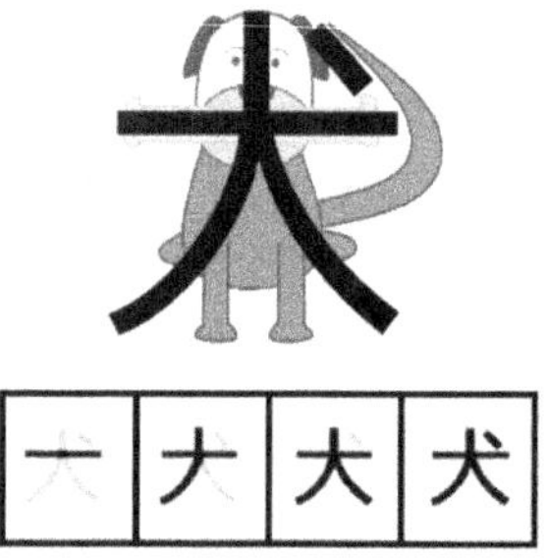 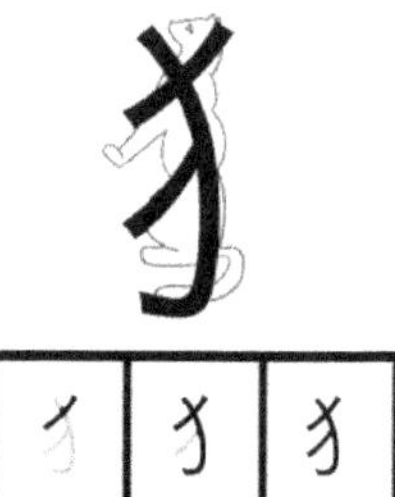

Try it:

FIRE 火 灬

The radical for **"fire"** (火 /灬) is a symbol of energy, transformation, and warmth. It is a crucial radical for understanding characters related to cooking, light, and intensity.

Known as 火 **ひ** (*hi*) or 灬 **れっか** (*rekka*), this radical is another very clear pictogram. The central strokes represent the main body of a fire, while the two outer strokes represent the sparks and flames flickering upwards. When the fire is placed at the bottom of a character, it is flattened into four dots to provide a stable base for the rest of the *kanji*.

When you see this radical, it is all about the heat!

1. **Literal Fire and Heat:**

    - 焼 (やく – to burn/roast): Using **fire** (火) on the left to cook or char something.

WATHC OUT! Animal Shapes (The "False" Fire): In some characters, the four dots have nothing to do with the fire radical! They are "simplified" versions of animal parts.

    - 馬 (うま – horse): The four dots represent the **four legs** and the **mane** of the horse running.

    - 鳥 (とり – bird): The dots represent the **feet**.

    - 魚 (さかな – fish): The dots represent the **fins** or the tail moving in the water.

FIRE

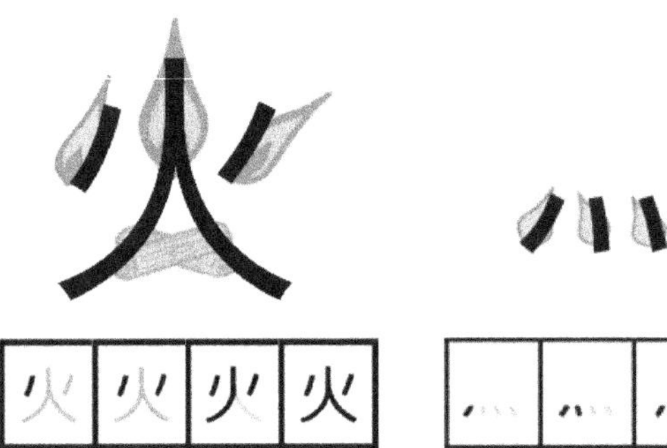

Try it:

KING 王

The radical for **"king"** (王) holds a prestigious position in the writing system. However, it is a "dual-purpose" radical. While the stand-alone *kanji* means king, when it appears on the left side of a character, it almost always represents **jade** or **precious stones**.

Known in Japanese as **おう** (*ou*) or **たま** (*tama*), this radical has a deep philosophical origin. One popular theory is that the three horizontal lines represent **Heaven** (top), **Earth** (bottom), and **Man** (middle). The vertical line is the "King" who connects all three.

Historically, the *kanji* for "King" was 王 and "Jade" was 玉. To make writing faster, the dot in "Jade" was dropped when it moved to the left side. Therefore, if you see 王 on the left, your first thought should be **"precious stone,"** not "emperor."

Because jade was the most precious substance in ancient East Asia, this radical defines beauty, value, and order.

1. **Jewelry and Gemstones:**

   - 珠 (たま – pearl/gem)

   - 球 (きゅう – ball/sphere)

2. **Governance and Authority:**

   - 理 (り – logic/justice): Originally, this character meant "to polish jade."

KING

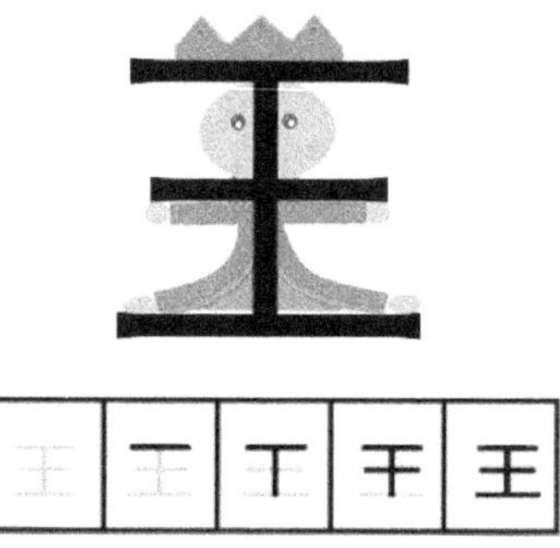

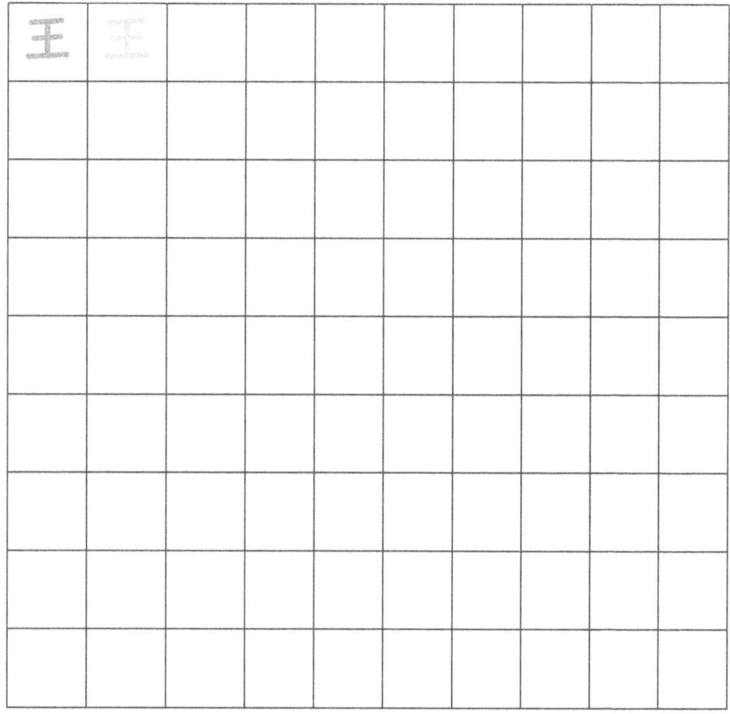

Try it:

RICE PADDY 田

The radical for **"rice paddy"** (田) is a fundamental pictogram that serves as the blueprint for ancient economic and social life. Because land ownership was synonymous with survival and power, this radical appears in characters related to labor, geography, and even deep thought.

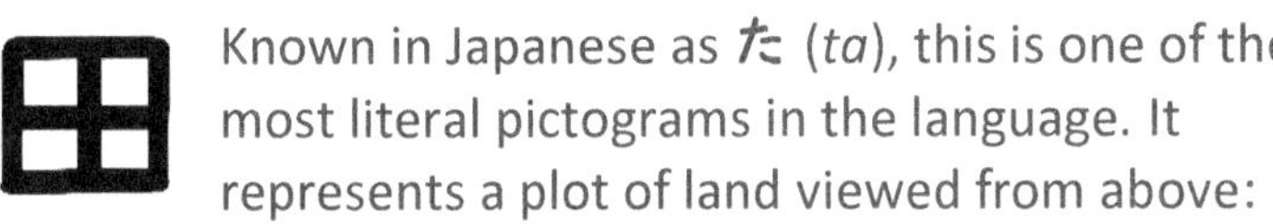

Known in Japanese as *た* (*ta*), this is one of the most literal pictograms in the language. It represents a plot of land viewed from above: The horizontal and vertical lines in the center represent the **ridges** (narrow paths) that separated different farmers' plots and the **irrigation ditches** used to flood the fields.

When 田 appears as a radical, it typically categorizes *kanji* into these three areas:

1. **Landforms and Agriculture:**

   - 畜 (ちく – livestock): Originally represented the storage of food produced by the **field** (田).

2. **Fieldwork and Human Agency:**

   - 男 (おとこ – man): The combination of **field** (田) and **strength** (力).

3. **Location and Boundaries:**

   - 町 (まち – town): Combines **field** (田) with a **nail** (丁). It represents the place where fields are marked out and people settle.

RICE PADDY

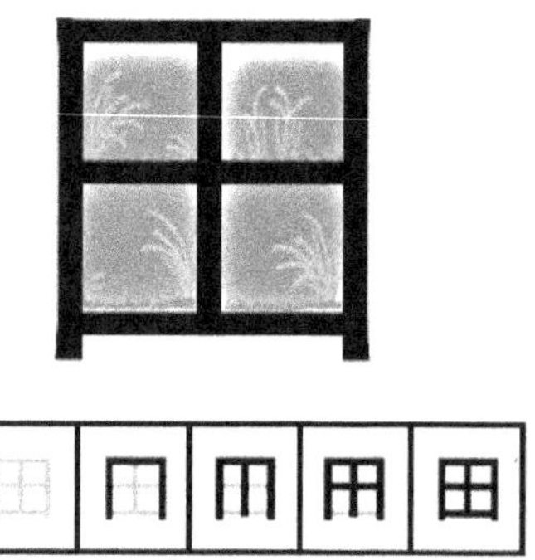

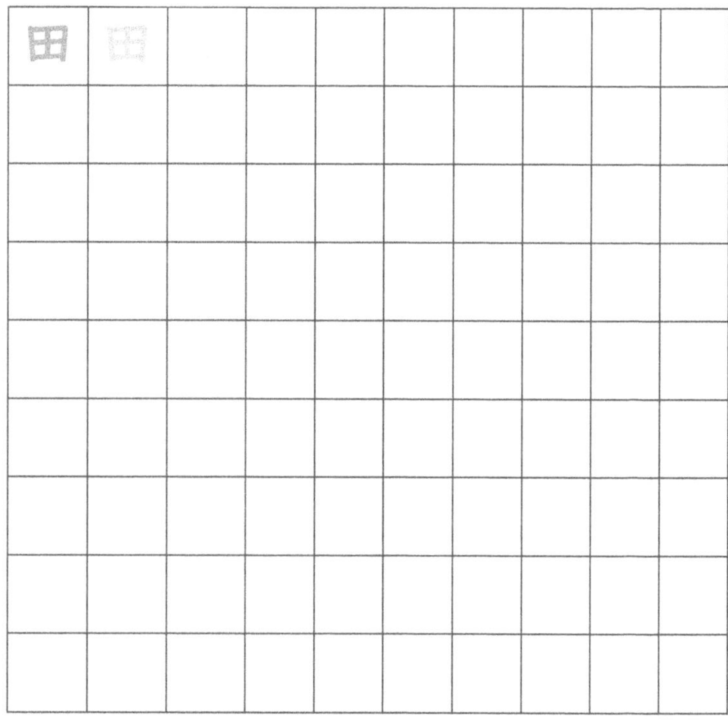

Try it:

ILLNESS 疒

The radical for **"illness"** (疒) is the "hospital" of the Japanese writing system. It specifically represents disease, pain, or physical discomfort. By studying this radical, we see how ancient people viewed the vulnerability of the human body.

Known in Japanese as やまいだれ (*yamaidare*), this radical is a vivid pictogram of someone in distress. The vertical stroke and the "shelf" on the left represent a **bed.** The top strokes represent a **person leaning** or lying against that bed because they are too weak to stand on their own.

When you see radical, the *kanji* almost always falls into one of these three medical categories:

1. **Damage to Bodily Functions:**

   - 病 (びょう – illness): The most common character for sickness.

2. **Specific Physiological Manifestations:**

   - 疲 (つかれる – to be tired/fatigued): Originally meant being so weary it felt like an illness.

3. **Cognitive and Mental States:**

   - 痴 (ち – foolish/stupid): Historically viewed as a "sickness of the mind" or a lack of clarity.

   - 癒 (いえる – to heal/cure): This radical can also be used for the **recovery** process from illness.

119

ILLNESS

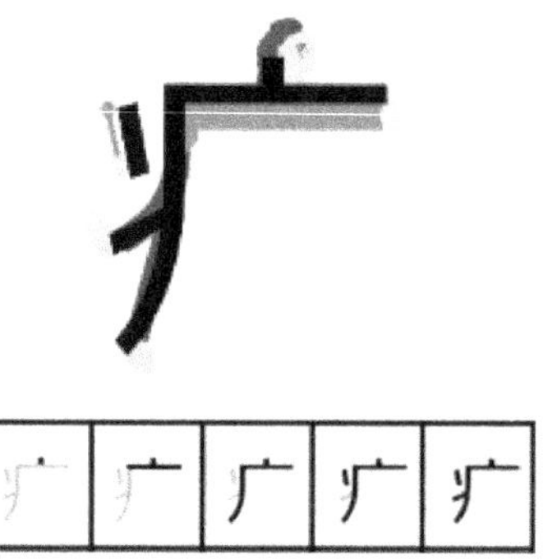

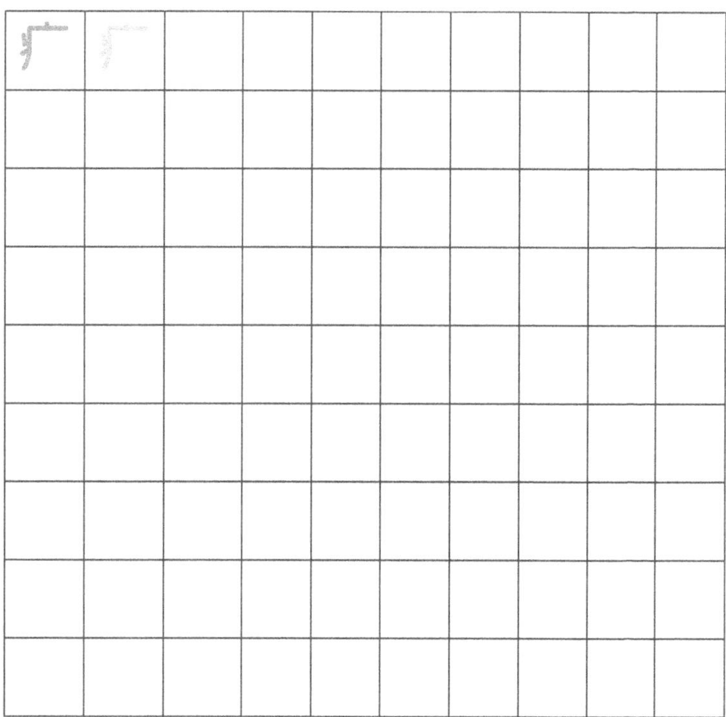

Try it:

DISH 皿

The radical for **"dish"** (皿) is a classic pictogram that provides a glimpse into ancient dining and ritual culture. It doesn't just represent household objects; it carries connotations of containment, and abundance.

Known in Japanese as さら (*sara*), this radical is a literal drawing of a container. The horizontal line at the top represents the **wide rim** of a vessel, the two vertical lines in the middle show the **interior walls**, and the horizontal line at the bottom represents the **base**. While it may look simple today, it originally represented the elaborate bronze vessels or high-quality pottery used during the Zhou Dynasty for both daily meals and sacred offerings.

When 皿 appears as a radical, it usually indicates one of the following two areas:

1. **Serving and Containing:**

    - 盆 (ぼん – tray/basin): A container used to hold or carry things.

2. **Actions involving Vessels:**

    - 盗 (ぬすむ – to steal): Interestingly, this shows a person "drooling" (次) over a **dish** (皿), symbolizing the desire to take what belongs to someone else.

    - 益 (えき – benefit): Depicts water overflowing from a **dish** (皿), representing surplus and gain.

DISH

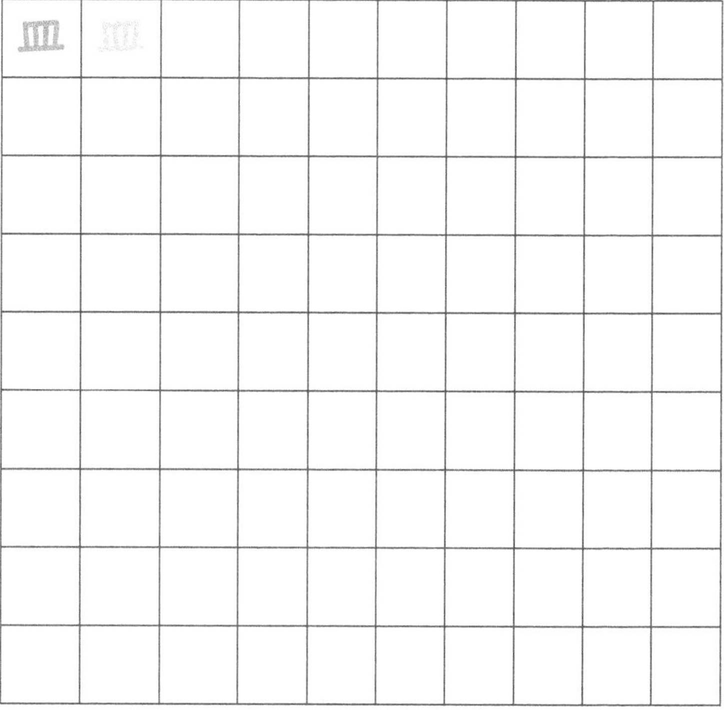

Try it:

EYE 目

The radical for **"eye"** (目) is one of the most expressive components in Japanese. It acts as a "lens" for the character, signaling that the meaning involves vision, tracking, or the physical state of the eye itself.

Known as め (*me*), this radical is a direct descendant of a physical drawing. Originally, this was an oval shape drawn horizontally with a pupil in the center. As the writing system evolved to be more compact and uniform, the eye was "stood up" vertically. The outer rectangle represents the **eye socket**, and the two horizontal lines inside represent the **pupil and iris**.

When 目 appears in a *kanji*, it typically directs the meaning toward one of these three categories:

1. **Vision and Physical Characteristics:**

   - 盲 (もう – blind): A "deceased" (亡) **eye** (目).

2. **The Action of Looking:**

   - 眺 (ながめる – to stare): Using the **eye** (目) to look at the "prospect" or "omen" (兆).

3. **Abstract Perception and Truth:**

   - 真 (しん – truth/reality): Historically related to seeing things as they truly are.

   - 瞬 (しゅん – blink/instant): The time it takes for an eye (目) to perform a quick movement.

EYE

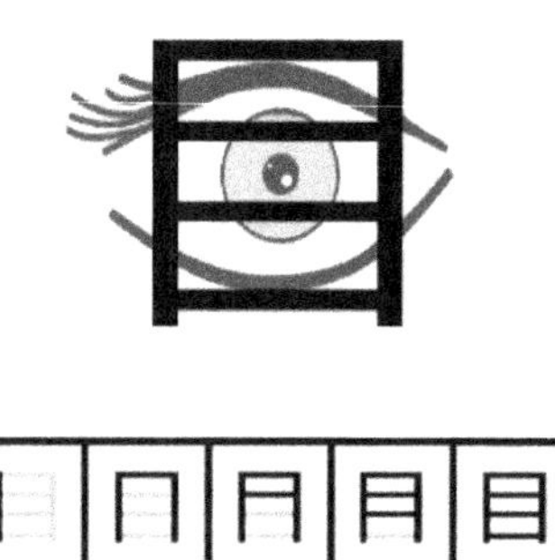

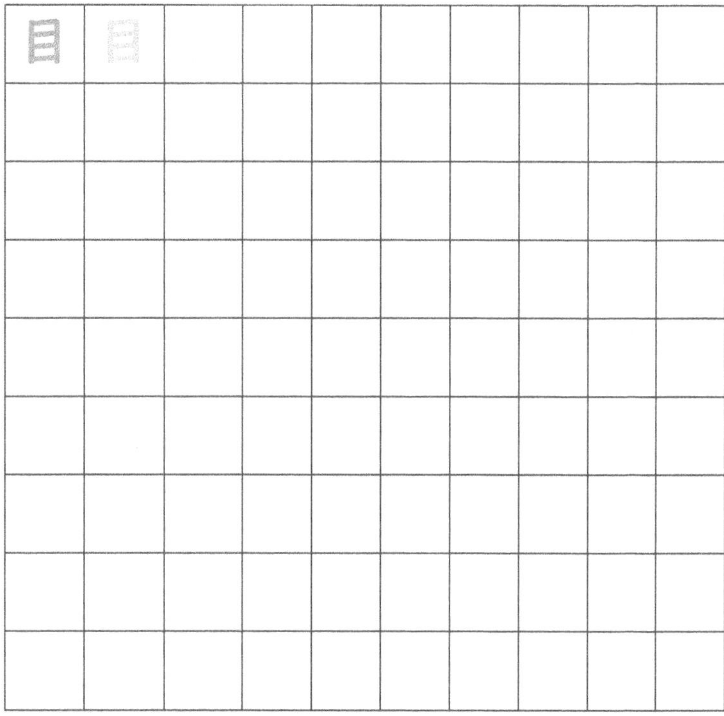

Try it:

STONE 石

The radical for **"stone"** (石) is a foundational element in *kanji* that denotes minerals, masonry, and the physical properties of solid objects. Because stones were the primary tools and building blocks of early civilization, this radical appears in everything from ancient weaponry to modern scientific terms.

Known in Japanese as いし (*ishi*), this radical is a structural pictogram. The top part (厂) represents a **cliff**. The bottom part looks like the character for "mouth" (口), but it actually represents a **rock** sitting at the base of that cliff.

When 石 appears in a character, it usually anchors the meaning in one of these three categories:

1. **Natural Forms and Geology:**

    *   岩 (いわ – rock/boulder): A "mountain" (山) made of **stone** (石).

2. **Tools and Technology:**

    *   硯 (すずり – inkstone): The stone block used to grind ink for calligraphy.

    *   砲 (ほう – cannon): Before gunpowder, cannons were catapults that threw **stones** (石).

3. **Physical Properties:**

    *   硬 (かたい – hard/stiff): The primary quality of a **stone** (石).

STONE

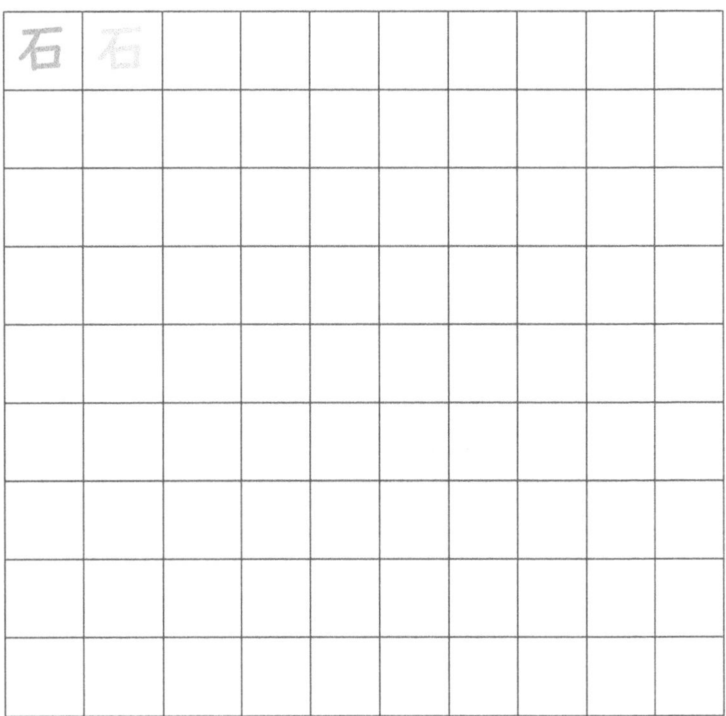

Try it:

ALTAR 示 ネ

The radical for **"altar"** (示 / ネ) is one of the most culturally significant components in *kanji*. It connects the human world to the realm of spirits, gods, and fate.

Known in Japanese as **しめす** (*shimesu*), this radical is a pictogram of a sacrificial altar. The horizontal strokes at the top represent the **surface** where offerings were placed. The vertical and diagonal lines below represent the **pillars**. Ancient people believed that by making offerings on this altar, the gods would reveal their will. This is why the radical eventually came to mean "to show".

When you see ネ, the *kanji* almost always involves the supernatural or the spiritual:

1. **Deities and Spirits:**

    - 神 (かみ – god): An **altar** (ネ) and "lightning" (申), representing a god.

2. **Sacrificial Activities and Rituals:**

    - 祭 (まつり – festival): Shows "meat" and a "hand" over an **altar** (示).

3. **Fortune, Luck, and Prayer:**

    - 祝 (いわい – celebrate): A "person" (儿) with a "mouth" (口) praying at an **altar** (ネ).

    - 祈 (いのる – to pray): Using an altar (ネ) and an "axe" (斤). Praying before war.

ALTAR

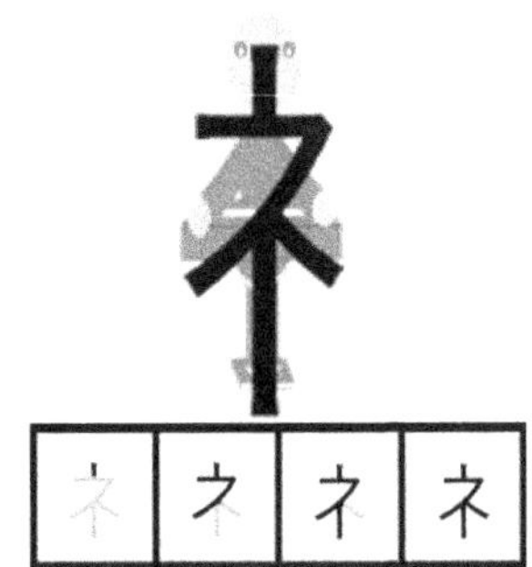

Try it:

GRAIN 禾

The radical for **"grain"** (禾) is a vital category that points to the core of ancient agricultural civilization. While the "Rice Paddy" (田) represents the land itself, the "Grain" radical represents the **crop**—the life-giving product of the soil.

Known in Japanese as *のぎ* (*nogi*), this radical is a beautifully clear pictogram that depicts a stalk of grain (specifically millet). **The Top Slash** represents the heavy, ripened "ear" of the grain drooping downward. **The Middle** shows the upright stem. **The Bottom** is the root system anchoring the plant.

When 禾 appears, it usually signals that the *kanji* is related to one of these three social or physical categories:

1. **Crops and Botanical Growth:**

   - 穂 (ほ – ear/head of grain): The flowering part of the plant.

2. **Harvest and Seasons:**

   - 秋 (あき – autumn): The **grain** (禾) is ready to be dried or "fired" (火) after the harvest.

3. **Measurements, Math, and Systems:**

   - 税 (ぜい – tax): Literally "exchanging" your **grain** (禾) with the government.

   - 程 (ほど– extent/degree): Originally a measurement of grain.

GRAIN

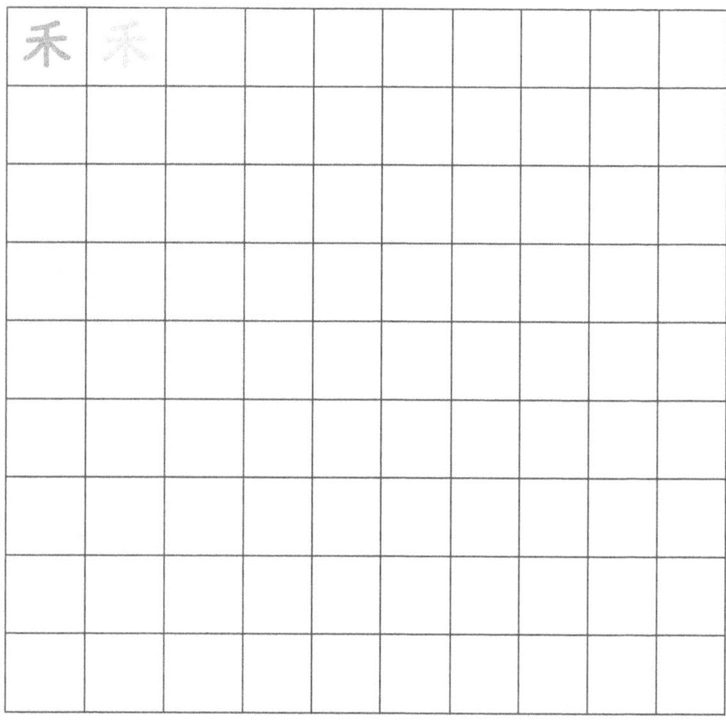

Try it:

HOLE 穴

The radical for **"hole"** (穴) follows a remarkably unified and intuitive logic. It is the primary symbol for caves, burrows, and any action performed through an opening. Because early humans were "cave dwellers", this radical preserves the memory of our first homes.

Known in Japanese as **あな** (*ana*), this radical is a clear architectural pictogram. The top part represents the "ceiling" of a cave, and two diagonal strokes at the bottom represent the sides of the **opening**. Like this, it depicts a hollow space carved into a mountain or the ground.

When 穴 appears at the top of a character, it usually categorizes the meaning into one of these three areas:

1. **Architecture and Space:**

   - 空 (そ ら – sky/empty): Essentially, the vast emptiness of the sky.

   - 窓 (ま ど – window): Historically, a hole (穴) made to let smoke and light pass through.

2. **Actions and Physical Force:**

   - 穿 (う が つ – to drill/pierce): The action of making a hole in something.

3. **Abstract States of Emptiness:**

   - 窪 (く ぼ む – become depressed): A sunken place in the ground.

HOLE

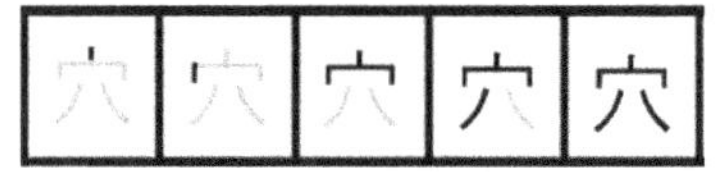

Try it:

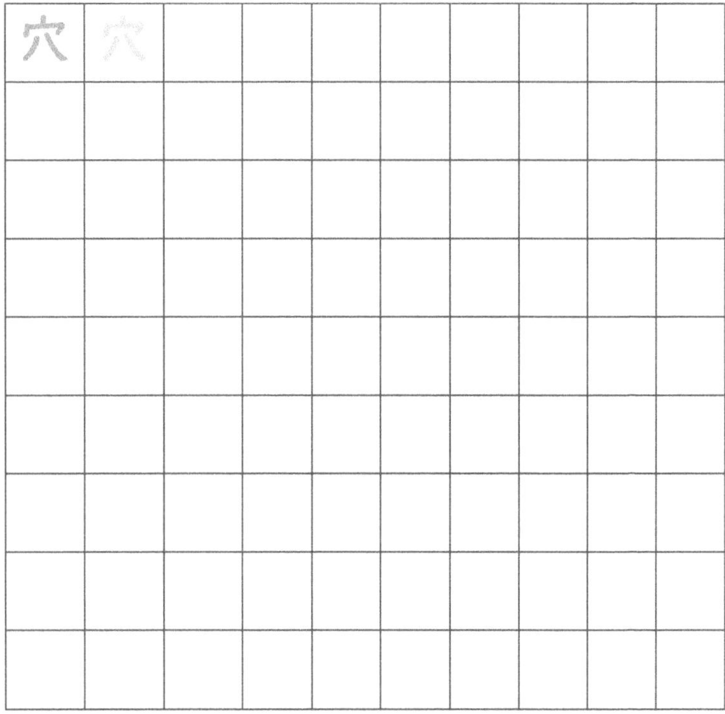

STANDING 立

The radical for **"stand"** (立) is a powerful pictogram that captures the moment a person rises to their feet. It has evolved from a simple physical motion into a profound metaphor for independence, social rules, and the setting up of structures or ideas.

 Known in Japanese as **たつ** (*tatsu*), this character is a direct representation of a human profile. The **top dot** represents the head, the **horizontal line** below it represents the shoulders, the **two diagonal strokes** represent the legs, the **bottom horizontal line** represents the ground. It shows a person firmly planted on the earth, emphasizing **stability** and **willpower**.

When 立 appears in a character, it usually directs the meaning toward one of these two categories:

1. **Physical Stance and Orientation:**

    *   競 (きそう – compete): Shows two "standing" people side-by-side, as if at the starting line of a race.

    *   端 (はし – edge/end): A person "standing" (立) at the very edge of a point.

2. **Establishment:**

    *   章 (しょう – chapter/badge): Originally related to a "mark" that was "established" to show rank or achievement.

STANDING

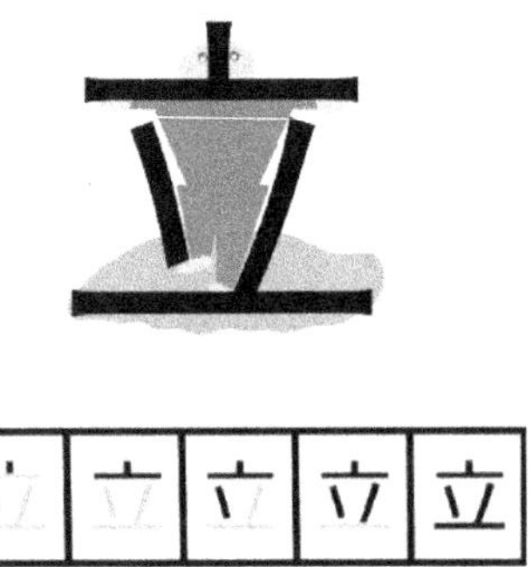

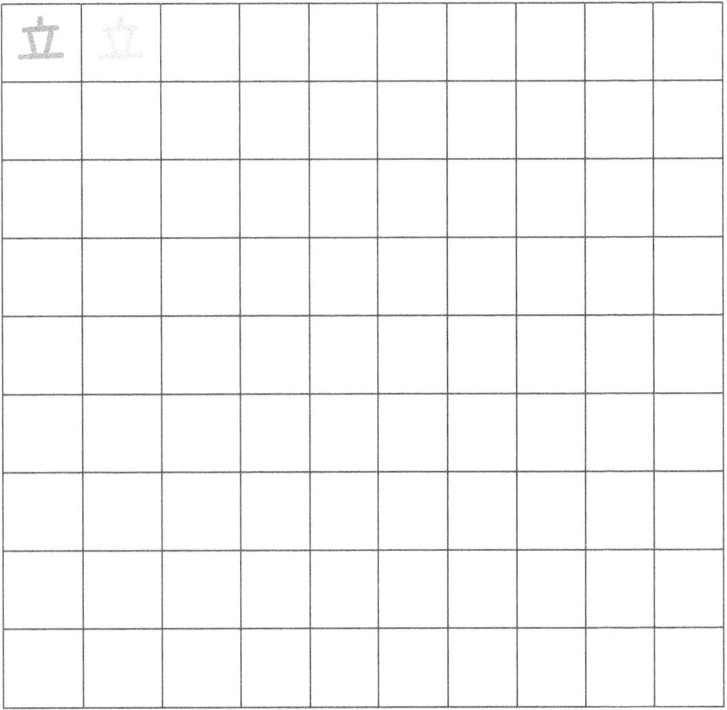

Try it:

BAMBOO 竹

The radical for **"bamboo"** (竹 / ⺮) is a culturally significant category. Because bamboo grows rapidly and is both strong and flexible, it was the primary material for ancient technology, record-keeping, and art. If a character contains this radical, it almost always refers to an object traditionally crafted from this "wonder-plant."

Known in Japanese as **たけ** (*take*), this radical is a beautiful pictogram. It depicts two stalks of bamboo side-by-side. The small diagonal strokes at the bottom of each "stalk" represent the **slender**, **drooping leaves** characteristic of bamboo forests. To fit at the top of a *kanji*, the stalks are flattened, looking like "tent-like" structures ⺮.

When ⺮ appears at the top of a character, it generally flows into these three categories:

1. **Writing and Record-Keeping:**

   - 筆 (ふで – writing brush): A **bamboo** (⺮) handle with a **hand** (聿) at the bottom.

2. **Daily Utensils and Containers:**

   - 箸 (はし – chopsticks): The most common bamboo tool in the household.

3. **Musical Instruments:**

   - 笛 (ふえ – flute)

BAMBOO

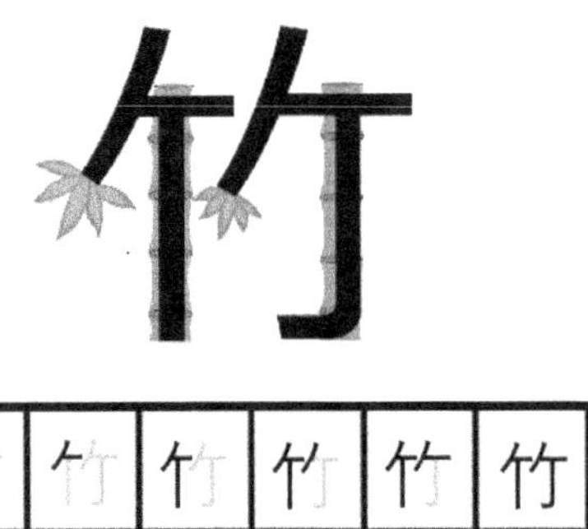

Try it:

RICE 米

The radical for **"rice"** (米) is a foundational component that records the agricultural heartbeat of the ancient world. It constructs a fascinating semantic network ranging from the literal grain to its physical properties.

Known in Japanese as こめ (*kome*), this radical is a highly symmetrical pictogram, representing several scattered grains of rice: The **horizontal and vertical cross** in the middle represents a sieve used to separate the grain from the husk, or the stalks of the plant. The **four diagonal dots** represent the individual grains of rice being threshed or scattered.

Unlike the radical for "Grain" (禾), which represents the living plant in the field, 米 specifically refers to the **kernels** after they have been harvested and shelled.

When 米 appears in a character, it usually categorizes the meaning into one of these two areas:

1. **Grain Types and Processing:**

   - 粉 (こな – flour/powder): A **grain** (米) that has been "divided" (分) into tiny pieces.

2. **Physical Properties:**

   - 粗 (あらい – coarse/rough): Originally referred to unpolished, low-quality rice.

   - 粧 (しょう – cosmetics): In ancient times, face powder was made from finely ground rice flour.

RICE

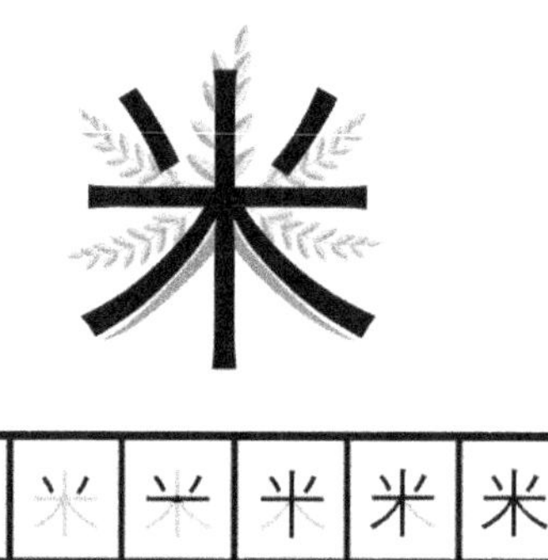

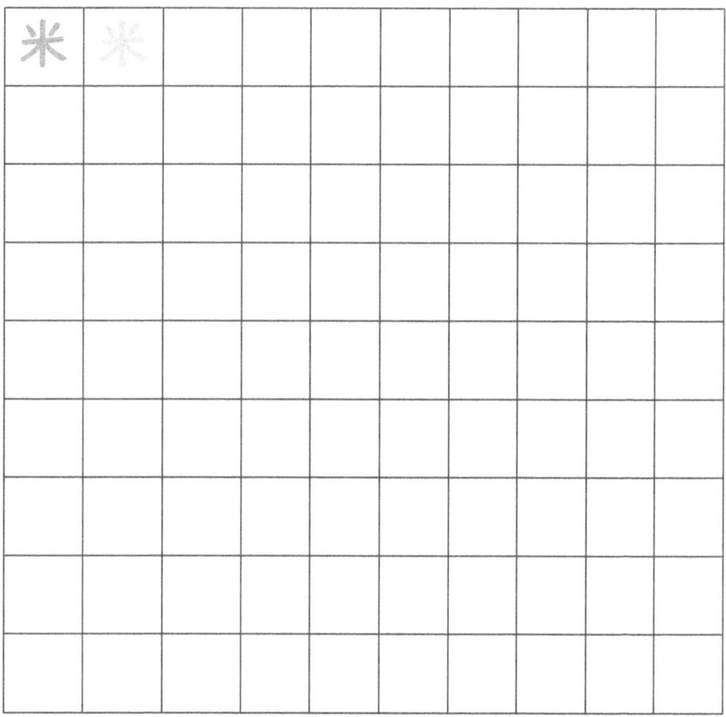

Try it:

THREAD 糸

The radical for **"thread"** (糸) is one of the most prolific in the Japanese language. It highlights the profound importance of ancient textiles—specifically silk. It weaves a semantic network that spans from the literal creation of cloth to the abstract "connection" of people.

Known in Japanese as いと (*ito*), this radical is a detailed pictogram of raw fiber. The top part represents a **loop or a twist of silk** being pulled from a cocoon. The bottom part originally depicted the **loose, fraying ends** of the thread.

When 糸 appears, you are usually looking at one of these four categories:

1. **Materials and Textiles:**

   - 綿 (めん – cotton)

2. **Colors and Dyes:** Color was primarily experienced through dyed silk threads.

   - 緑 (みどり – green): Originally referred to the color of dyed silk.

3. **Connection and Continuity:**

   - 結 (むすぶ – to tie/conclude)

4. **Lines and Organization:**

   - 線 (せん – line)

THREAD

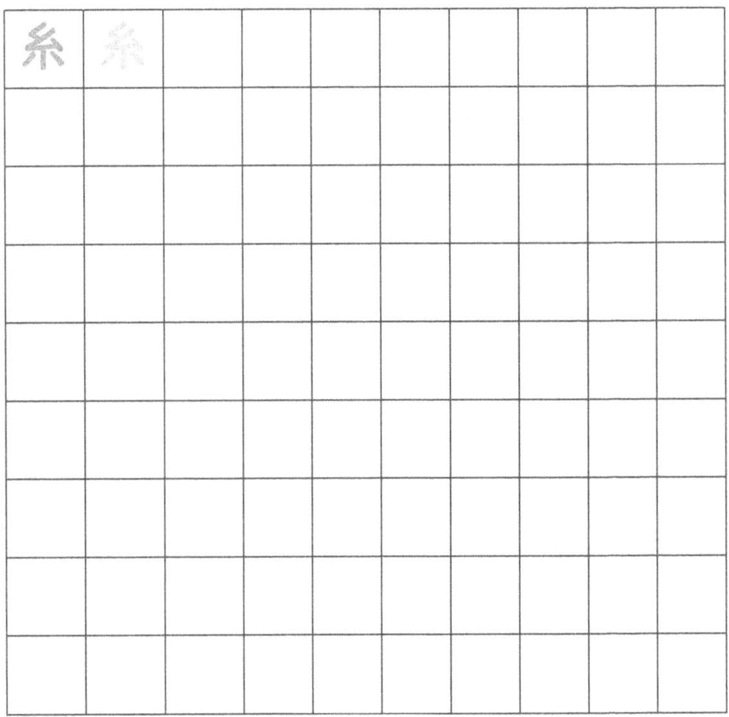

Try it:

NET 罒

The radical for **"net"** (罒) is a unique and versatile component. While it began as a literal tool for catching birds and fish, the meaning expanded to represent the "legal net" of the state, including capture, restriction, and punishment.

Known in Japanese as **あみがしら** (*amigashira*), this radical is a simplified version of the ancient character 网. The horizontal rectangle with the vertical bars inside represents a **woven net** held open by a frame or ropes. Because nets are often cast from above, this radical always sits at the top of a *kanji*. For ease of writing and to maintain the balance of the character, the vertical net was turned on its side.

When 罒 appears, it generally signals that the character involves one of these two themes:

1. **Literal Tools and Netting:**

   - 羅 (ら – gauze/thin silk): Originally a net for catching birds, now used for fine fabric.

2. **The Legal Net (Crime and Punishment):**

   - 罪 (つみ – crime/guilt): Historically, this showed a **net** (罒) catching a "wrong" (非) act.

   - 置 (おく – to place/set): Originally meant to "catch and set aside." It depicts a **net** (罒) and "straight/correct" (直).

NET

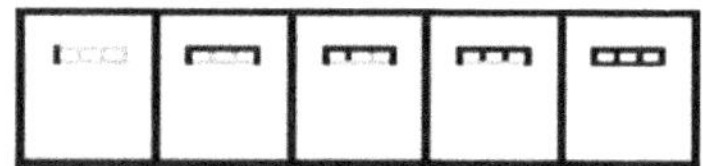

Try it:

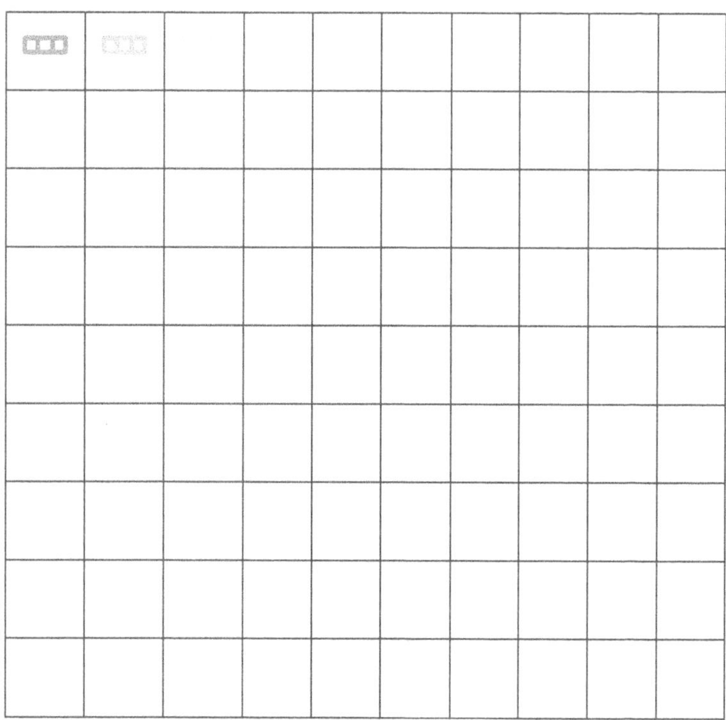

SHEEP 羊

The radical for **"sheep"** (羊) is a pillar of aesthetics and ethics in the *kanji* system. Because sheep were docile, high-value livestock, and the preferred animal for sacred rituals, they became a metaphor for everything "good," "beautiful," and "righteous."

 Known in Japanese as ひつじ (*hitsuji*), this radical is a classic frontal pictogram. Like the Cow radical (牛), this depicts the head of the animal from the front. The **top strokes** (ゝ✓) represent the horns, but unlike the cow's upward horns, these traditionally curve downward. The **three horizontal lines** represent the ridges of the face and ears. The **vertical line** represents the bridge of the nose.

When this radical sits at the top of a character, the bottom vertical stroke is often shortened or removed (⺷) to make room for the component below.

When 羊 appears, it usually signals a connection to one of these two cultural pillars:

1. **Aesthetics and Morality:**

   - 美 (うつくしい – beauty): A "large" (大) **sheep** (羊). In ancient times, a big, healthy sheep was the very definition of "beautiful."

2. **Social Behavior and Groups:**

   - 群 (むれ – flock): A **sheep** (羊) and a "lord" (君). It describes a flock following a leader.

SHEEP

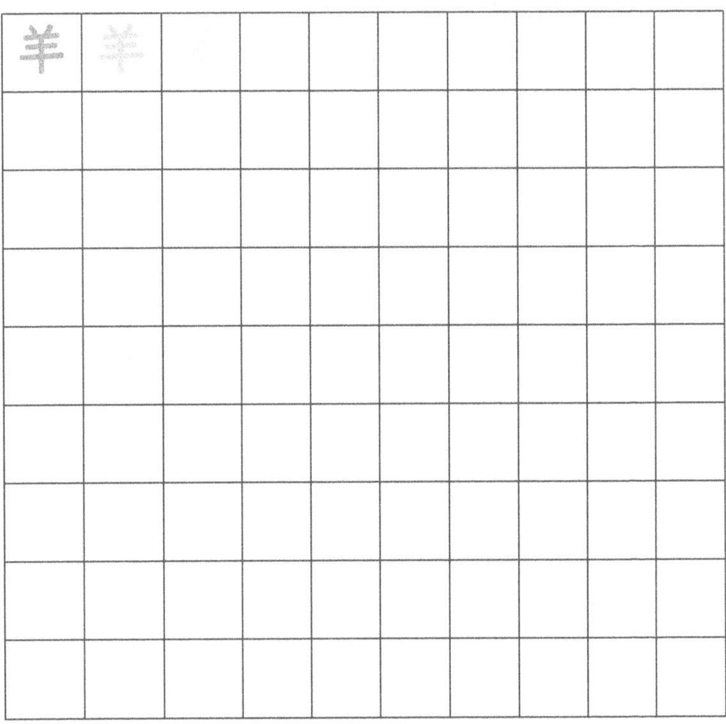

Try it:

FEATHERS 羽

The radical for **"feathers"** (羽) is the "aviation" radical of the Japanese language. It categorizes characters related to birds, flight, and the materials made from plumage. Beyond physical birds, it also represents the concept of **repetition** and the pursuit of mastery.

Known in Japanese as **はね** (*hane*), this radical is a symmetric pictogram. It depicts a pair of wings side-by-side. The outer "frames" are the quills, and the short strokes inside represent the soft barbs of the feather.

When 羽 appears in a character, it usually signals one of these three themes:

1. **Feathers and Avian Anatomy:**

   - 翼 (つばさ – wing): The most literal use, describing the limb used for flight.

   - 翠 (すい – kingfisher): Named after the brilliant "blue-green" feathers of the kingfisher bird.

2. **The Action of Flight and Practice:**

   - 習 (ならう – to learn): It shows "wings" (羽) over "white/sun". It represents a **young bird flapping its wings** to learn how to fly.

3. **Abstract States:**

   - 翌 (よく – the next/following): Related to the "folding" of wings or the passage of time.

FEATHERS

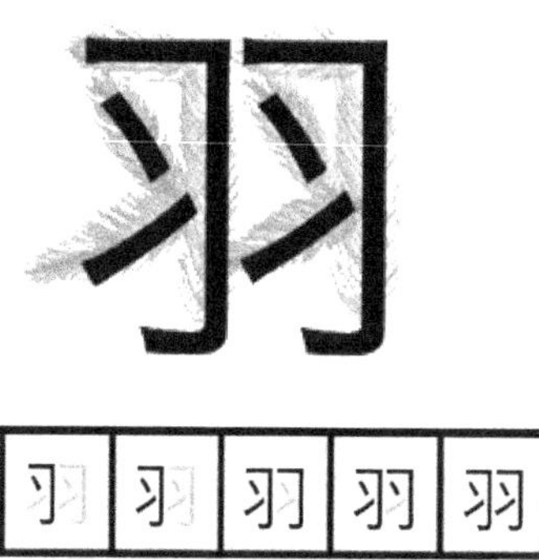

Try it:

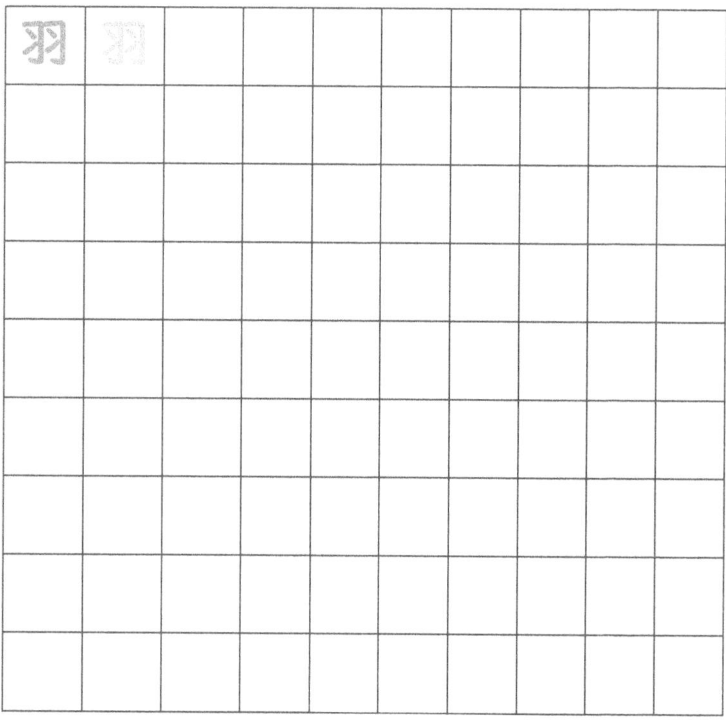

FLESH 肉 月

The radical for **"flesh"** (肉/月) is the primary building block for the human body. While it started as a drawing of a piece of meat, it evolved to look identical to the "Moon" (月) radical. Because of this, it is known in Japanese as に くづき (*nikudzuki*)—literally, the "Meat-Moon." However, when this radical appears on the left or bottom of a character, it almost always represents anatomy, not moon.

The original pictogram for 肉 showed a slice of meat with the **ribs or fibers** visible inside. To make characters more balanced, the "meat" was squeezed into the shape of a moon. In ancient scripts, the two middle lines of the "meat" version were slanted (月), but in modern Japanese, they look exactly the same (月).

When you see 月, the *kanji* usually falls into one of these two biological categories:

1. **Body Parts and Organs:**

   - 肌 (はだ – skin): The "surface" of the **flesh** (月).

   - 背 (せ – back): Two "people" standing back-to-back (北) over the flesh (月).

2. **Biological Development and Actions:**

   - 育 (そだつ – to grow/rear): Shows a child being born/nourished by the **flesh** (月).

FLESH

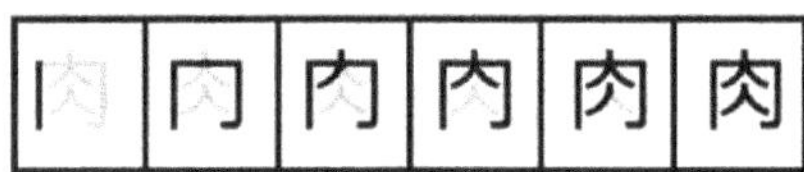

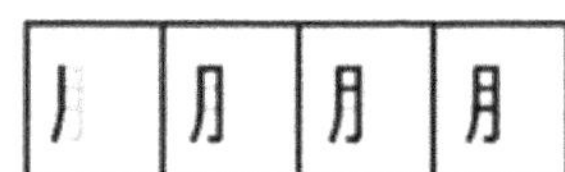

Try it:

BOAT 舟

The radical for **"boat"** (舟) is a highly intuitive component. It acts as the "nautical" marker for the Japanese language, recording not only the evolution of transportation but also the ancients' deep connection to life on the water.

Known in Japanese as **ふね** (*fune*), this radical is a literal drawing of a vessel. It depicts a long, narrow boat (like a dugout canoe) viewed from an angle. The **outer frame** represents the hull with its upturned bow and stern. The **inner horizontal lines** represent the internal benches or the "ribs" of the boat. The **dots** (often written as a slanted stroke in the center) represent either the contents of the boat or the oars used for propulsion.

When 舟 appears, it usually anchors the character in one of these two maritime categories:

1. **Types and Names of Vessels:**

    *   船 (ふね – large ship): This is the most common use. It combines "boat" (舟) with a component meaning "marsh" or "flowing," referring to a vessel built for larger waters.

    *   艦 (かん – warship): A **boat** (舟) that acts as an "official" (監).

2. **Navigation and Movement on Water:**

    *   航 (こう – navigate): A **boat** (舟) "crossing" (亢) the water.

BOAT

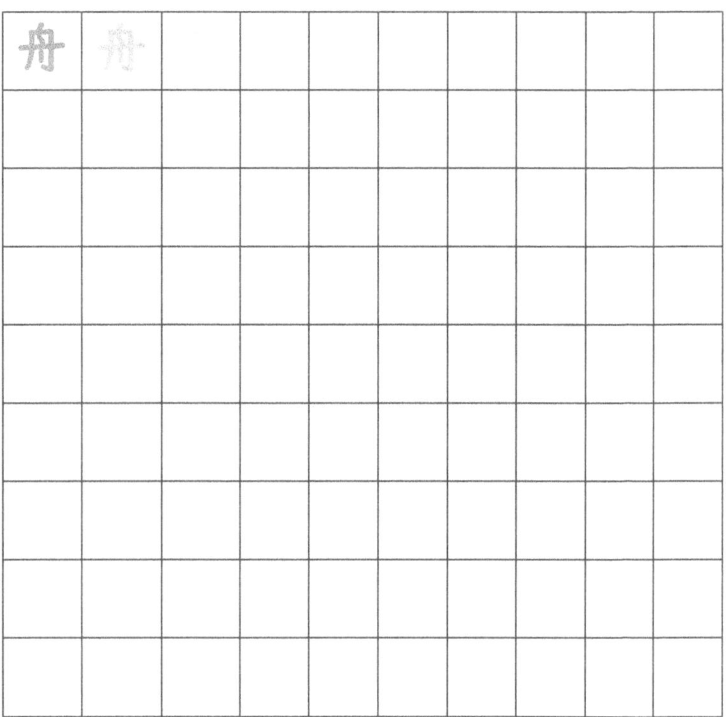

Try it:

GRASS 艹

The radical for **"grass"** (艹) has one of the clearest evolutionary lineages in the *kanji* system. It is the primary marker for the plant kingdom, herbal medicine, and the cycle of growth.

Known in Japanese as くさ (*kusa*), this radical began as a drawing of life pushing through the soil. Originally, the radical consisted of two separate sprouts side-by-side (艸). Each one looked like a tiny fork (屮) representing a stem and two leaves. For the sake of speed and neatness, the two sprouts were connected by a single horizontal bar, creating the three or four-stroke "crown" we see today.

When 艹 appears at the top of a character, it usually categorizes the meaning into one of these three areas:

1. **Plant Names and Food:**

    - 芋 (いも – potato/tuber)

2. **Plant Parts and Growth Stages:**

    - 花 (はな – flower): A plant (艹) that "changes" (化) as it blooms and withers.

3. **Human Behavior and Sensations:**

    - 苦 (くるしい – suffering): Ancient medicines were made from **plants** (艹), and they were **old** (古) and bitter. This evolved into the meaning of "hardship."

GRASS

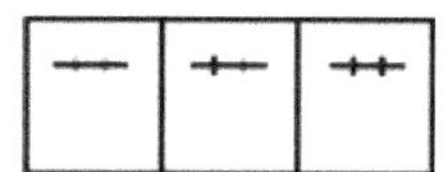

Try it:

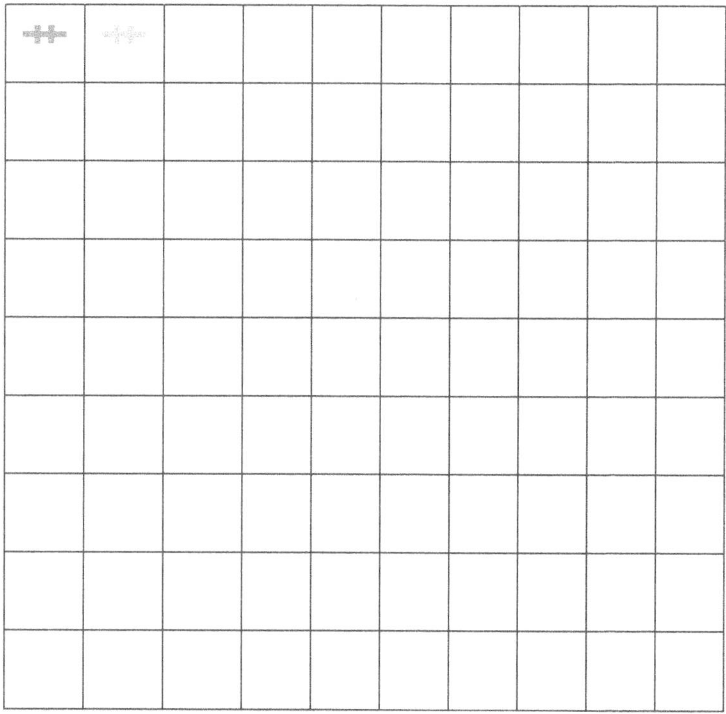

INSECT 虫

The radical for **"insect"** (虫) is the "biological grab-bag" of the Japanese language. While we call it the "insect" radical today, its ancient scope was much broader, including reptiles, amphibians, and even some natural phenomena that were thought to be living spirits.

Known in Japanese as むし (*mushi*), this radical has a surprising origin: it is a pictogram of a snake. The top "box" represents the **head of a snake**, and the curved stroke below represents its **winding body**. While the original character for a general "bug" was 蟲, over time, this was simplified to the single 虫 we use today.

Because the ancients didn't have modern biological classifications, 虫 appears in characters for a wide variety of "small creatures":

1. **True Insects and Arthropods:**

   - 蚊 (か˴ – mosquito): An insect (**虫**) that makes a "bun" (**文**) sound (the buzzing noise).

2. **Small Non-Insect Animals:**

   - 蛇 (へび – snake): Returning to its roots, a **creature** (虫) that is "long/slithering."

   - 蛙 (かえる – frog): A **creature** (虫) that "croaks."

INSECT

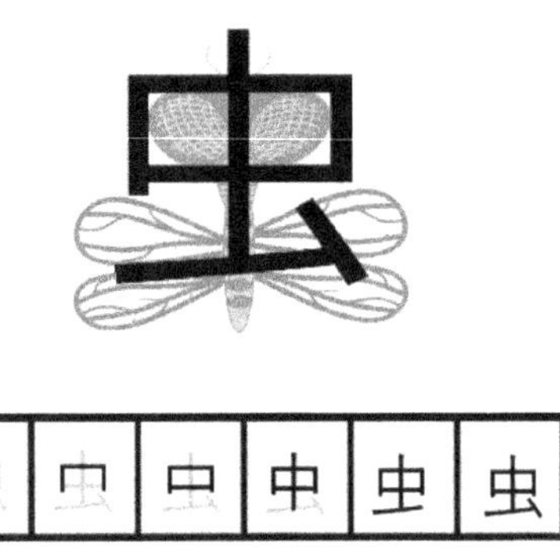

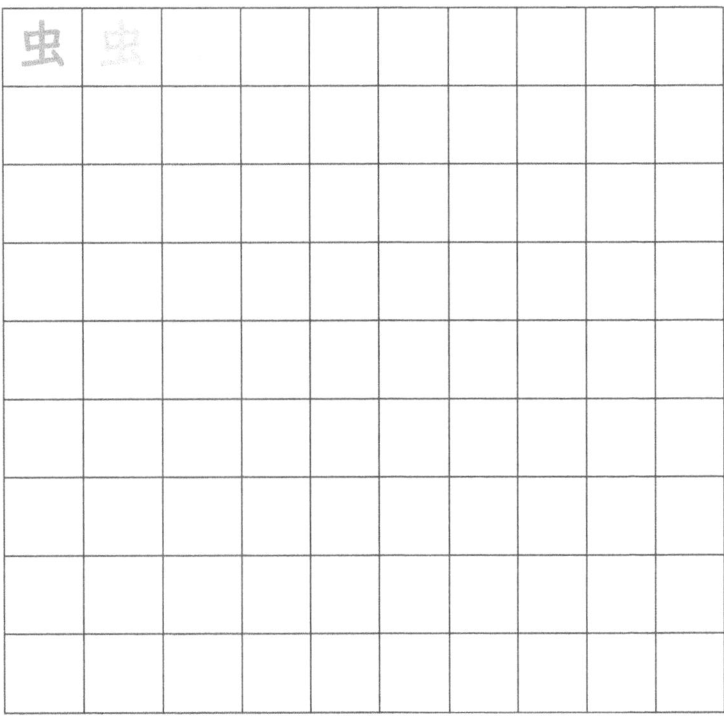

CLOTHING 衣 ネ

The radical for **"clothing"** (衣/ネ) provides a fascinating look at ancient fashion and social hierarchy. While it originally referred specifically to an "upper garment" (like a robe), it expanded to cover anything made of fabric, as well as the concepts of "covering" or "hiding" something.

Known in Japanese as **ころも** (*koromo*), this radical is a classic pictogram of a traditional garment. The top part (亠) represents the **collar and neck** of the robe. The bottom part (𧘇) represents the **sleeves and the hem** of the garment as it hangs down. Then, when the radical moves to the left side, it simplifies to ネ.

When you see this radical, the *kanji* usually falls into one of these three categories:

1. **Names and Parts of Clothing:**

   - 袖 (そで – sleeve): One of the most recognizable parts of a kimono.

2. **Function and Manufacturing:**

   - 装 (そう – attire/dress): To "establish" one's **clothing** (衣).

3. **Abstract and Extended Meanings:**

   - 表 (おもて – surface): Originally depicted a fur garment worn with the fur on the **outside**.

CLOTHING

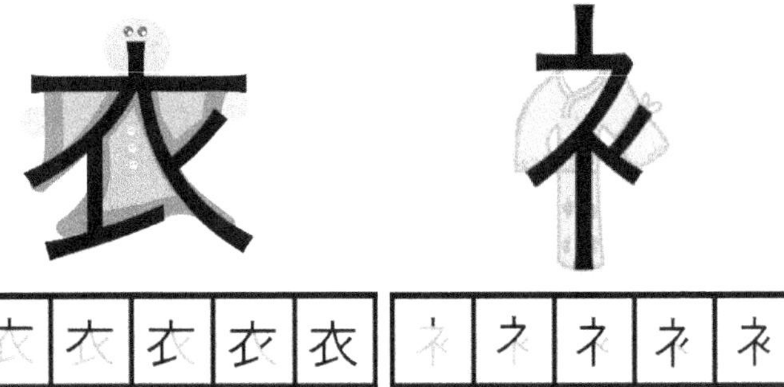

Try it:

EAR 耳

The radical for **"ear"** (耳) is a highly intuitive and symbolic component. Beyond representing the physical auditory organ, it has evolved to represent the acts of listening, gathering information, and even achieving a high social or spiritual status through "hearing" the truth.

Known in Japanese as *みみ* (*mimi*), this radical is a literal drawing of the human ear. The vertical lines represent the **outer curve (auricle)** of the ear, while the horizontal lines represent the **inner ridges and the ear canal**. In *kanji*, the ear isn't just for hearing sounds; it's for **understanding** and **recording** knowledge.

When 耳 appears in a character, it usually directs the meaning into one of these two categories:

1. **Hearing and the Senses:**

   - 聴 (きく – to listen): To truly listen, you must give your ear and your whole heart.

2. **Wisdom and Assistance:**

   - 聡 (さとい – wise): Originally meant "keen hearing," but evolved to mean someone who is "sharp-witted" because they listen well.

   - 職 (しょく – employment): In ancient courts, a "duty" often involved listening to and documenting official matters.

EAR

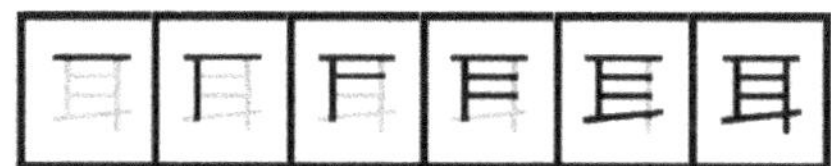

Try it:

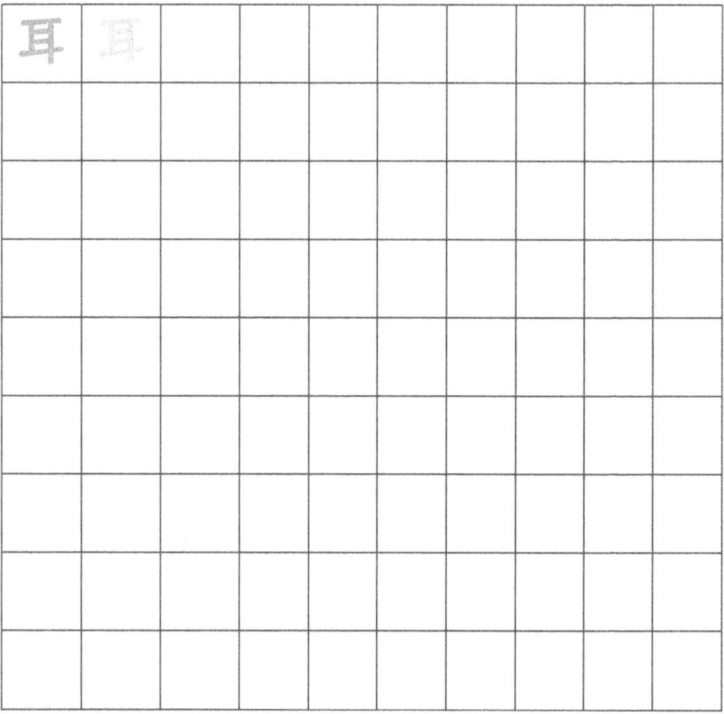

TIGER 虍

The radical for **"tiger"** (虍) is a highly distinctive component commonly known as the **"Tiger Head."** More than just a symbol, it embodies the ancient observation and awe of the tiger—the king of the mountains and forests. It often marks characters related to strength, cruelty, or intense physical struggle.

Known in Japanese as **とらがしら** (*toragashira*), this radical is a vivid pictogram of the tiger's upper body. The **top horizontal stroke and hook** represent the ears and the top of the head. The **vertical and diagonal strokes** represent the tiger's stripes.

When 虍 appears, it usually categorizes the *kanji* into one of these two powerful themes:

1. **The Literal Tiger:**

   - 虎 (とら – tiger): The most basic form, adding the "legs" (儿) to the tiger head.

2. **Power, Cruelty, and Conflict:**

   - 虐 (しいたげる – oppress): Shows a **tiger** (虍) with its **claws** (ヨ) out.

   - 虜 (りょ – captive): Depicts a **tiger** (虍) and a **man** (男).

TIGER

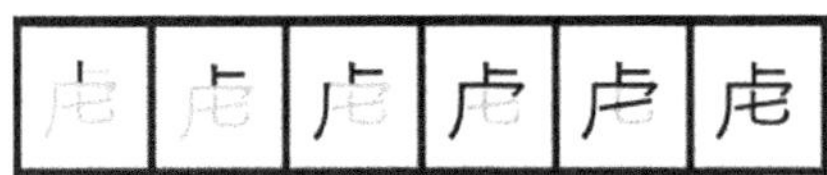

Try it:

JOURNEY 行

The radical for **"journey"** (行) is both a high-frequency *kanji* and a vital radical. Known in Japanese as **ぎょう** (*gyō*) or **ゆきがまえ** (*yukigamae*), it provides the structural framework for characters involving movement, streets, and the "ways" in which we perform skills.

This radical is a literal map. It is a pictogram of a **crossroad** or a T-junction viewed from above. The **left part (彳)** represents a "left step" or the left side of a street. The **right part (丁)** represents a "right step" or the right side of a street. Together, they represent a path where people go to and fro. When this radical "wraps" around another component, it suggests that the action is happening **on the road** or is part of a **process**.

When 行 appears, it usually anchors the character in one of these two categories:

1. **Roads and Urban Space:**

   - 衝 (つく – collide)

2. **Technique and "The Way":**

   - 術 (じゅつ – technique/art): Originally referred to a path through a grain field, it evolved to mean the "path" or **method** one takes to master a skill.

   - 衛 (えい – defense/protection): To go **around** a road to keep it safe. It represents "guarding" a perimeter.

JOURNEY

Try it:

SEE 見

The radical for **"see"** (見) vividly demonstrates how the ancients constructed abstract concepts through human organs and their movements. It shifts the focus from the eye as a biological part to the act of **vision** as a human experience.

Known in Japanese as **みる** (*miru*), this radical is a clever "action-pictogram." It is composed of two distinct parts: The upper part is a large, wide-open eye 目. The lower part (written as 儿) represents the legs of a person. It depicts a person who has stopped in their tracks to look at something. By exaggerating the size of the eye on top of the legs, the ancients emphasized the **visual function**.

When 見 appears in a character (usually on the right side), it generally falls into one of these two categories:

1. **Direct Actions of Sight:**

   - 見 (みる – to see/view): The most basic form of the radical.

2. **Depth Observation and Regulation:**

   - 規 (き – standard): Originally showed a person using their **sight** (見) and a **compass** to set a standard.

   - 親 (おや – parent/intimate): A **parent** (親) watching over their children.

SEE

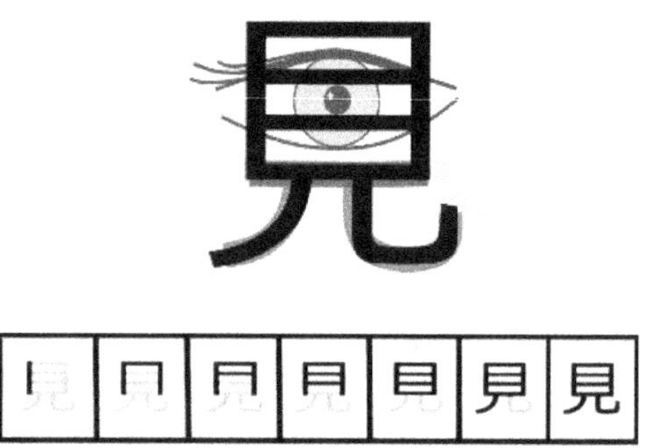

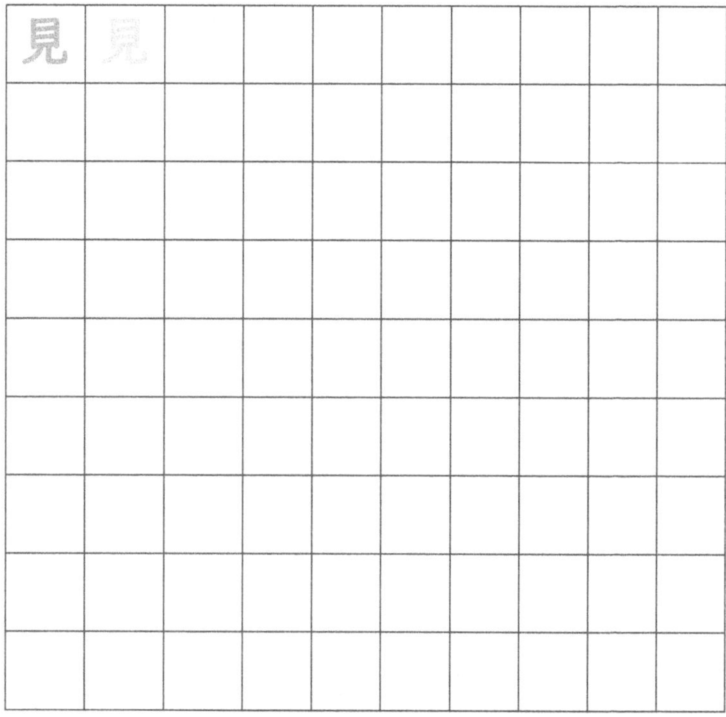

Try it:

SPEECH 言

The radical for **"speech"** (言) is one of the most prolific in the Japanese language. It marks the transition from thought to action. In a culture that values the "spirit of words", this radical covers everything from daily conversation to the sacredness of law.

Known in Japanese as ごんべん (*gonben*), this radical is a sophisticated pictogram of communication. It consists of two primary parts: The base represents the mouth 口, while the horizontal lines represented sound waves or the tongue. However, some scholars believe the top part represents a **tattooing needle**. In ancient legal rituals, a person would swear an oath; if they lied, they were "marked" with the needle.

When 言 appears, the character usually falls into one of these three categories:

1. **Manner and Behavior of Speaking:**

   - 評 (ひょう – evaluation/critique): Words (言) that are "leveled" (平).

2. **Laws, Oaths, and Restraints:**

   - 諾 (だく – consent/agreement): A formal "yes" or "all right" given through speech.

3. **Records and Literary Works:**

   - 詩 (し – poem)

SPEECH

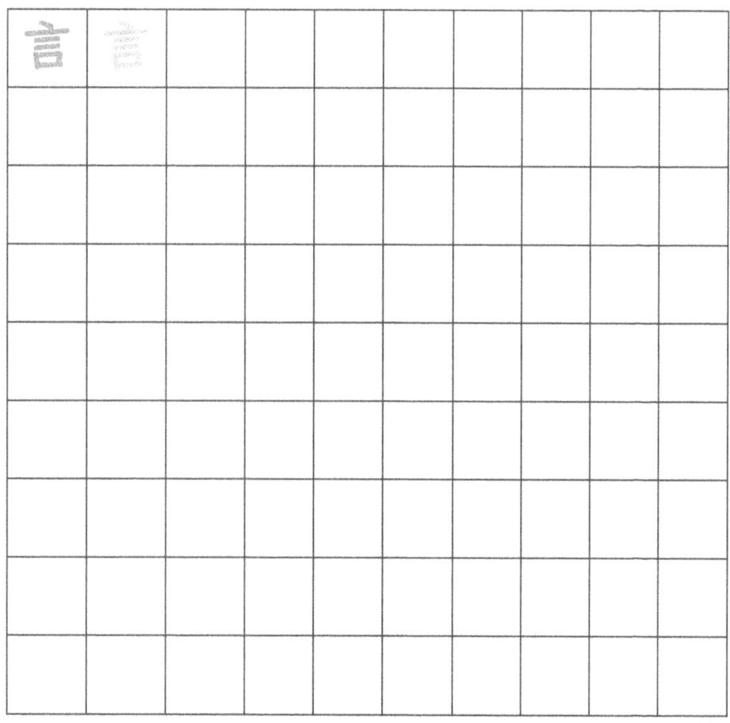

Try it:

SHELL 貝

The radical for **"shell"** (貝) holds a special place in the *kanji* system as the ancient symbol for value. Because cowry shells were the earliest form of currency in East Asia, this radical serves as a "money" marker, pointing toward wealth, trade, and the social weight of property.

Known in Japanese as **かい** (*kai*), this radical is a direct pictogram of a shellfish. The **upper rectangle** with the horizontal lines represents the body and the distinct patterns of a cowry shell. The bottom represents the "foot" of the shellfish peeking out from the shell.

When 貝 appears, it anchors the character in the world of economics and value:

1. **Property, Value, and Assets:**

    - 財 (ざい – wealth/assets): The "talent/ability" (才) to manage **money** (貝).

2. **Acquisitions and Transactions:**

    - 買 (かう – to buy)

3. **Rewards and Contributions:**

    - 賞 (しょう – prize/award)

4. **Debts and Negative Financial States:**

    - 負 (まける – defeat/lose/owe): To "bear a burden" over **money** (貝).

SHELL

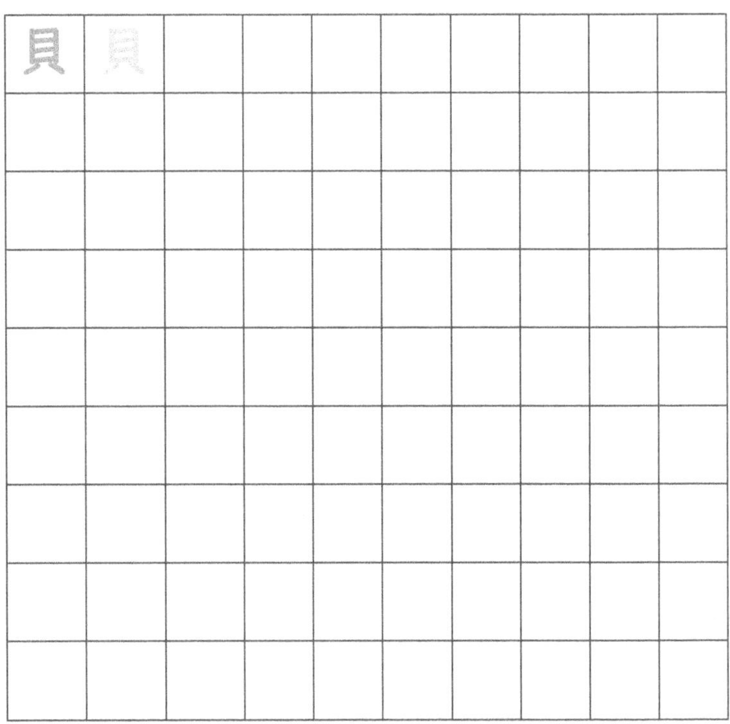

Try it:

LEG 足

The radical for **"leg"** (足) is a foundational component that records the ancients' observation of human anatomy and movement. It acts as the primary marker for any character involving the lower limbs, from literal body parts to complex actions like dancing or jumping.

Known in Japanese as **あし** (*ashi*), this radical is a vertical pictogram of a limb. It is traditionally viewed in two sections: **The Top** was originally a circle representing the **knee joint** or the thigh. **The Bottom** represents the **foot and toes**. You can see the heel and the toes pointing forward, suggesting a foot in motion.

When 足 appears, it usually categorizes the character into one of these three themes:

1. **Human Organs and Physicality:**

   - 足 (あし – foot/leg): The base character.

2. **Verbs of Motion and Action:**

   - 踊 (おどる – to dance)

   - 踏 (ふむ – to step on/tread)

3. **Traces and Results:**

   - 跡 (あと – trace/footprint/remains)

   - 路 (ろ – road/path): The place where the **foot** (足) "each/every" (各) person walks.

LEG

Try it:

CAR 車

The radical for **"car"** (車) is a significant and culturally rich component. It acts as the primary marker for transportation, mechanical movement, and military strategy. It records a time when the chariot was the "tank" of the ancient world, representing power and rotation.

 Known in Japanese as **くるま** (*kuruma*), this radical is a classic top-down pictogram. Imagine looking down at a chariot from the sky: The **top and bottom horizontal lines** represent the two large wheels. The **central box** represents the cabin where passengers or cargo sit. The **central vertical line** represents the axle connecting the wheels.

When 車 appears, it generally drives the character into one of these three categories:

1. **Vehicle Structures and Parts:**

   - 輪 (りん – wheel/ring): A **car** (車) part that is "circular" (侖).

2. **Movement and Rotation:**

   - 輸 (ゆ – transport): To move goods by **car** (車).

3. **Military and Power:**

   - 軍 (ぐん – army): A **car** (車) under a "cover" (冖). It represents a chariot-based encampment.

CAR

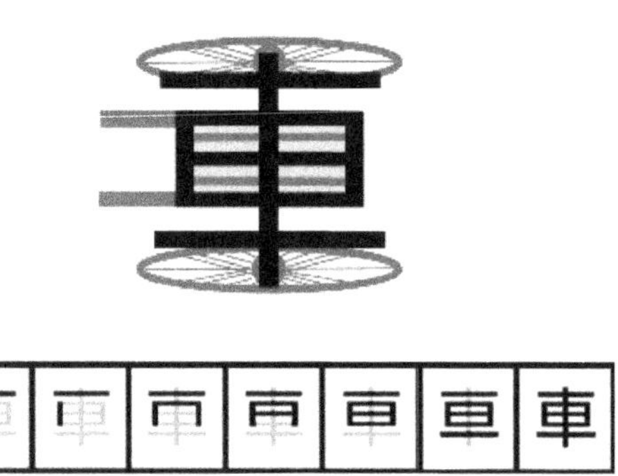

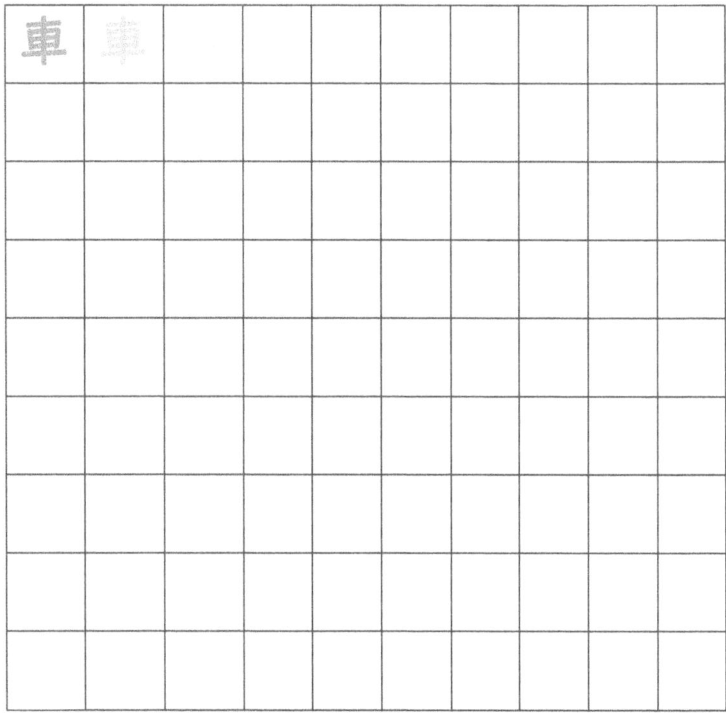

Try it:

TOWN 邑

The radical for **"town"** (邑 / 阝) is known as the "right ear radical" due to its modern shape, but its origin has nothing to do with hearing. It is a political radical, categorizing characters related to administrative districts, city limits, and the systems that keep a society running.

Known in Japanese as おおざと (oozato), it is a very clear radical, yet to understand it, we must look at its original form, 邑. **The Top** represents an enclosed territory or **city walls**. **The Bottom** represents a **kneeling person**. Together, they show a person residing within a defined territory, and the relationship between a land and its inhabitants. When this radical is used on the right side of a *kanji*, it is squeezed into the shape 阝 .

When you see 阝 on the **right**, the character usually relates to human-made borders and settlements:

1. **Administrative and Political Regions:**

   - 都 (と – capital/metropolis): A **town** (阝) where "many people" (者) gather.

2. **Outer Structures and Boundaries:**

   - 郊 (こう – suburbs/outskirts): A **town** (阝) that "crosses" (交) into the countryside.

   - 郵 (ゆう – mail/post): In ancient times, it referred to the **stops** along the road between **towns** (阝) where messengers could change horses.

TOWN

Try it:

ALCOHOL 酉

The radical for **"alcohol"** (酉) is a vessel of culture and science. It doesn't just represent drinking; it marks the entire process of **fermentation**, the creation of medicine, and even the passage of time in the ancient calendar.

Known in Japanese as **ひよみのとり** (*hiyominotori*), this radical is a detailed pictogram of a storage vessel. It depicts a ceramic jar with a narrow neck to keep air out and a wide belly for the liquid to settle. The horizontal lines inside the "belly" represent the liquid or the sediment of the fermenting grain.

When 酉 appears, the character can fall into one of these four areas:

1. **Types and States of Wine:**

    - 酒 (さけ– alcohol): All about adding the **"Water"** (氵) radical to the **"Jar"** (酉).

2. **Brewing and Fermentation:**

    - 酵 (こう – fermentation/yeast)

3. **Physical States After Drinking:**

    - 酔 (よう – drunk/tipsy)

4. **Tastes and Chemical Nature:**

    - 酢 (す – vinegar): Originally, vinegar was just wine that sat in the **jar** (酉) too long.

ALCOHOL

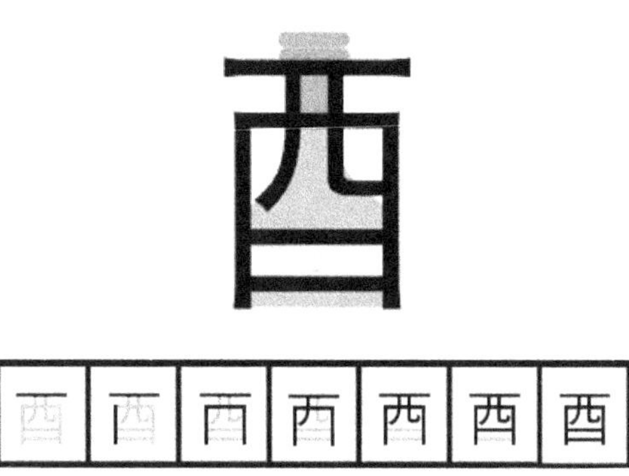

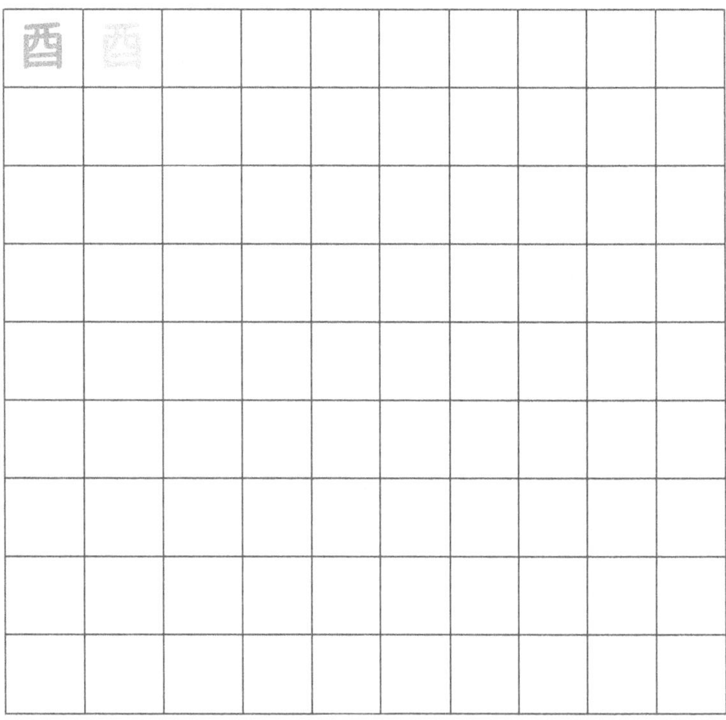

Try it:

METAL 金

The radical for **"metal"** (金)—often simply called the "Gold" radical—is one of the most powerful and common components in *kanji*. It marks everything from raw minerals and industrial tools to modern financial systems. It represents the strength, value, and utility of the earth's buried treasures.

Known in Japanese as **かね** (*kane*), this radical is a beautiful ideogram that tells a story of discovery. **The Top** part symbolizes **"containing"** or a "cover." **The Bottom** base is the character for **"Soil"**. The two diagonal dots represent the **nuggets of ore** hidden deep within that soil.

When 金 appears, it anchors the character in the world of physical materials and their worth:

1. **Metals and Raw Materials:**

   - 銀 (ぎん – silver)

2. **Processing Techniques:**

   - 鋳 (いる – to cast/mint)

3. **Objects and Tools:**

   - 針 (はり – needle)

4. **Value and Attributes:**

   - 銭 (せん – coin/small change)

METAL

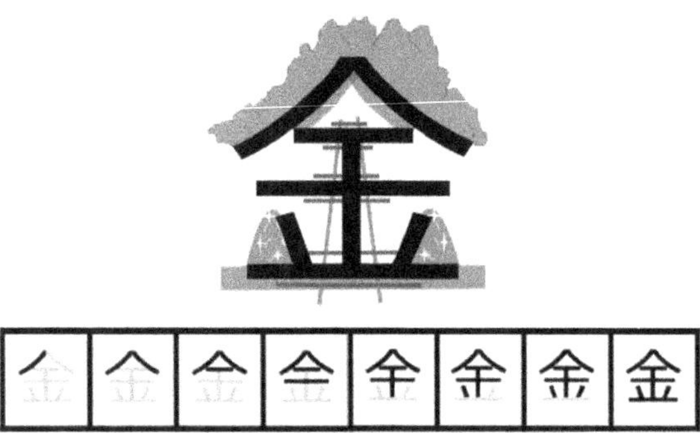

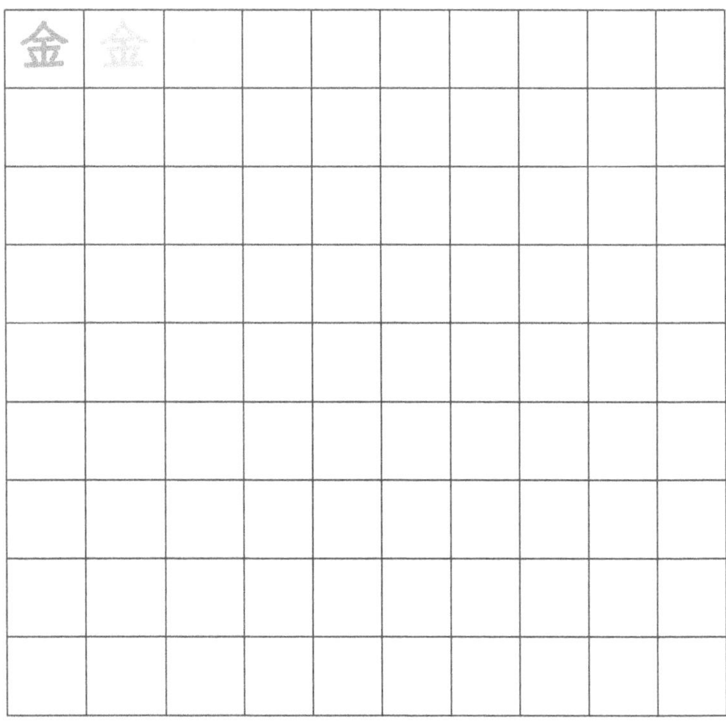

Try it:

GATE 門

The radical for **"gate"** (門) is a classic pictogram. Its structure profoundly reflects the form of ancient architecture, representing a grand, double-door entrance to a palace, a temple, or a courtyard. It acts as a "frame" radical, surrounding other components to define a space.

Known in Japanese as **もんがまえ** (*mongamae*), this radical depicts the standard double-entry gate of a traditional estate. The **two vertical pillars** represent the doorframes. The **horizontal and interior strokes** represent the two panels of the door that swing open. In *kanji*, the gate defines the boundary between the "inside" world and the "outside" world.

When 門 appears, it usually places the character into one of these three categories:

1. **Architectural Structures and Areas:**

   - 閣 (かく – tall building/palace): A **gate** (門) leading to a "high/sturdy" (各) structure.

2. **Space and Opening/Closing Actions:**

   - 開 (あける – to open): Showing hands lifting the "bolt" (开) of the **gate** (門).

3. **Abstract and Social Attributes:**

   - 闘 (とう – fight): Conflict happening within a confined space.

GATE

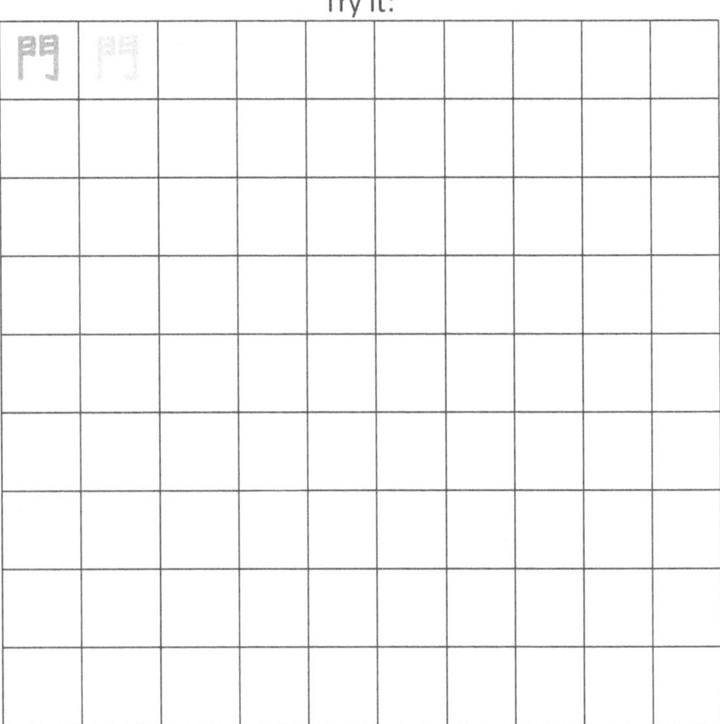

Try it:

MOUND 阜

The radical for **"mound"** (阜 / 阝) acts like a key, unlocking the ancient understanding of geographical space and elevation. It marks characters related to height, barriers, and the transition between different levels of land.

Known in Japanese as こざとへん (*kozatohen*), this radical is a pictogram of a steep cliff. The ancient shape (阜) looks like a vertical line with three "notches" or "bumps" on the side. These notches represent **steps** carved into a cliffside to help people climb up. When it sits on the left side of a character, it is compressed into the "left ear" shape (阝).

When you see 阝 on the **left**, the *kanji* usually falls into one of these three categories:

1. **Elevation and Terrain:**

   - 阪 (さか – slope/hill): A **mound** (阝) that is "opposed" (反).

2. **Man-made Barriers and Structures:**

   - 院 (いん – institution): Originally meant a courtyard surrounded by a **mound** (阝) for security.

3. **Abstract Height and Movement:**

   - 降 (ふる – descend): To come down from a **mound/height** (阝).

MOUND

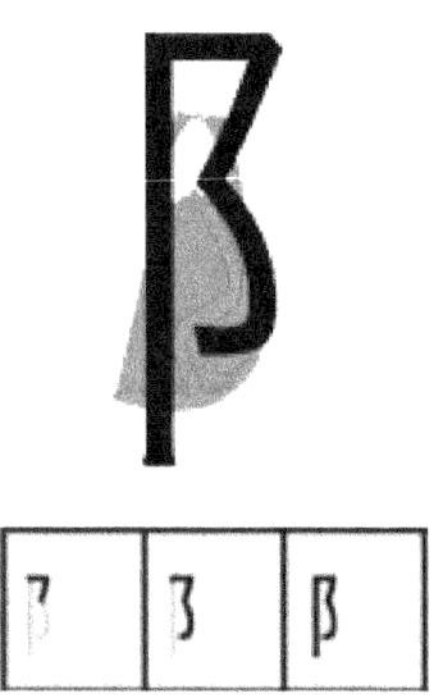

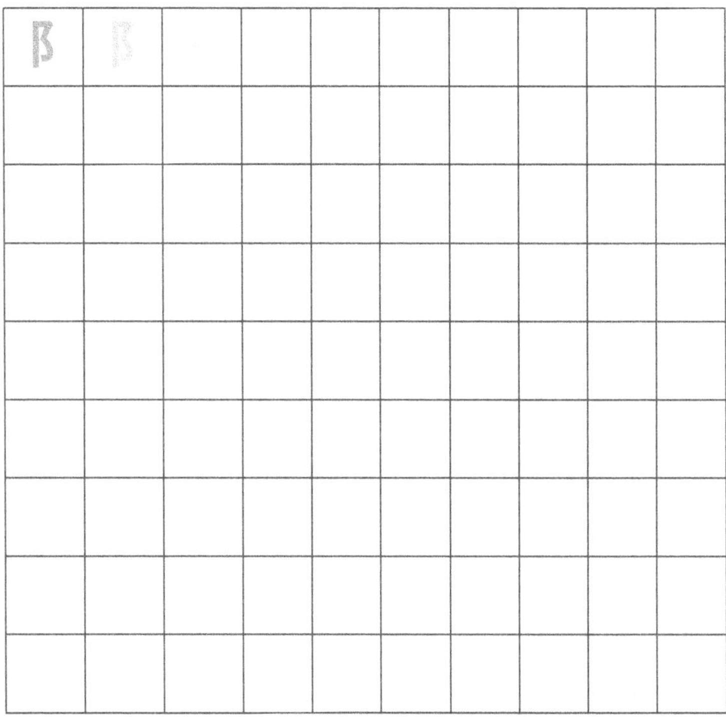

SMALL BIRD 隹

The radical for **"short-tailed bird"** (隹) unlocks a view into ancient ecology. Unlike the radical for "long-tailed birds" (鳥), 隹 focuses on the smaller, more compact birds. It appears in characters involving gathering, beauty, and even "difficulty"—reflecting the unpredictable nature of wild birds.

Known in Japanese as ふるとり (*furutori*), this radical is a classic profile sketch of a small bird. The **top slanted stroke** is the head and beak, the **vertical line** is the bird's back, and the **four horizontal strokes** represent the wing feathers and the short, stubby tail.

When 隹 appears, it usually categorizes the character into one of these three areas:

1. **Specific Bird Names:**

   - 雀 (すずめ – sparrow): A **small (小) bird (隹)**.

2. **Bird Behavior and States:** Actions inspired by birds.

   - 集 (あつまる – gather): Three **birds (隹)** sitting on a **tree (木)**. Think of birds gathering at dusk.

3. **Metaphor and Abstract Meanings:**

   - 難 (むずかしい – difficult): It originally represented a type of bird that was notoriously hard to catch, eventually becoming the general word for "difficulty."

SMALL BIRD

Try it:

RAIN 雨

The radical for **"rain"** (雨) is a primary marker for meteorology, astronomy, and natural phenomena. It provides a window into how ancient East Asian cultures understood the heavens—seeing weather as a force that could bring life to crops or destruction through storms.

Known in Japanese as **あめ** (*ame*), when it sits at the top, this radical is a vivid pictogram. The **top horizontal line** represents the wide expanse of the sky. The **outer frame** represents the clouds holding the moisture. The **four dots** are the literal water droplets falling to the earth.

When you see 雨 at the top of a *kanji*, it generally falls into these three categories:

1. **Weather and Atmospheric States:**

    - 雲 (くも – cloud): The "source" of the **rain** (雨).

2. **Natural Power and Sound:**

    - 電 (でん – electricity): Originally represented a bolt of lightning during a **rain** (雨) storm.

3. **Abstract and Measurement:**

    - 零 (れい – zero): Originally meant a very light, "fractional" **rain** (雨). Because it was so small, it eventually came to represent "nothing" or the number **zero**.

RAIN

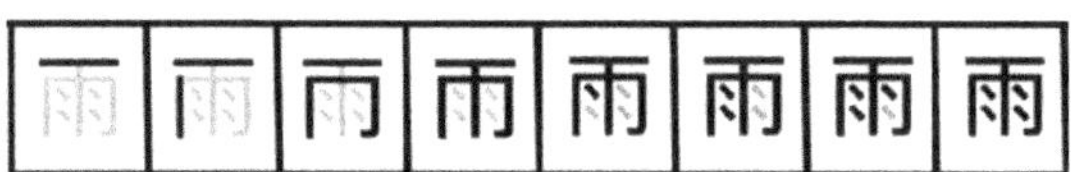

Try it:

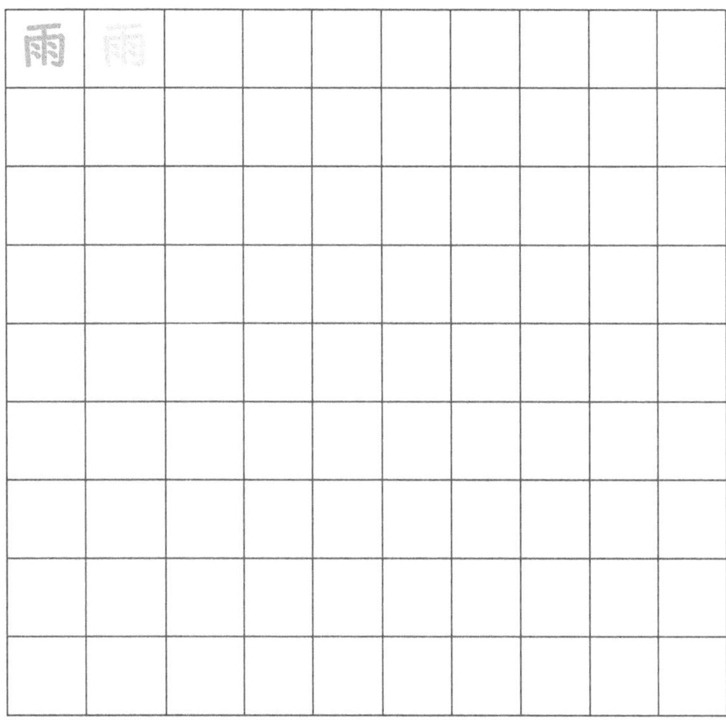

HEAD 頁

The radical for **"head"** (頁) is essentially an anatomical diagram. While many modern textbooks call it the **"page"** radical, its origins are strictly human. It marks characters related to the face, the neck, or cognitive actions where the head plays the starring role.

Known in Japanese as **おおがい** (*oogai*), this name literally means "Big Shell" because it looks like the shell radical, but with a different meaning. The **top horizontal line** and the **box** represent the hair and the face of a person. The **bottom part** represents a person kneeling on the ground. The ancients drew this character with an oversized head to emphasize that the "person" is defined by their **perception, face, or thoughts**.

When 頁 appears, it categorizes the *kanji* into these three areas:

1. **Parts of the Head and Neck:**

   - 顔 (かお – face): A combination of "colors/features" (彦) and the **head** (頁).

2. **Actions and Cognitive States:**

   - 顧 (かえりみる – look back): To turn the **head** (頁) to see what is behind you.

3. **Types and Classifications:**

   - 類 (るい – kind): Originally used to classify "heads" of animals or items.

HEAD

Try it:

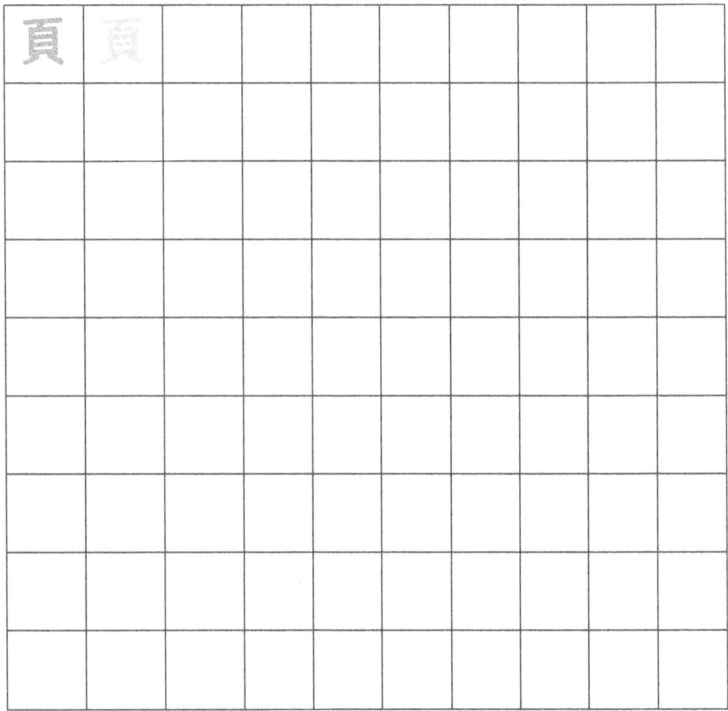

FOOD 食

The radical for **"food"** (食 / 食) is a fascinating window into ancient life. It doesn't just reflect what people ate, but the entire history of tableware and etiquette. It marks characters related to meals, the act of consuming, and the physical sensations of hunger and fullness.

 Known in Japanese as しょく (*shoku*), this radical is a detailed pictogram of a traditional meal. **The Top** represents an **inverted lid** or a cover. In ancient times, high-quality food was served in covered bronze or ceramic containers to keep the heat and aroma trapped inside. **The Bottom** represents a **food vessel** filled with grains. You can see the stable base at the very bottom and the "contents" in the middle. When this radical moves to the left side of a character, it is often simplified to 飠.

When 食 appears, it usually places the character into one of these three "culinary" categories:

1. **Types of Food and Meals:**

   - 飯 (めし – meal)

2. **Eating and Feeding Actions:**

   - 飲 (のむ – to drink): A person with an open **mouth** (欠) next to a **food/drink vessel** (食).

3. **Physical States and Sensations:**

   - 飢 (うえる – hunger/starve)

FOOD

Try it:

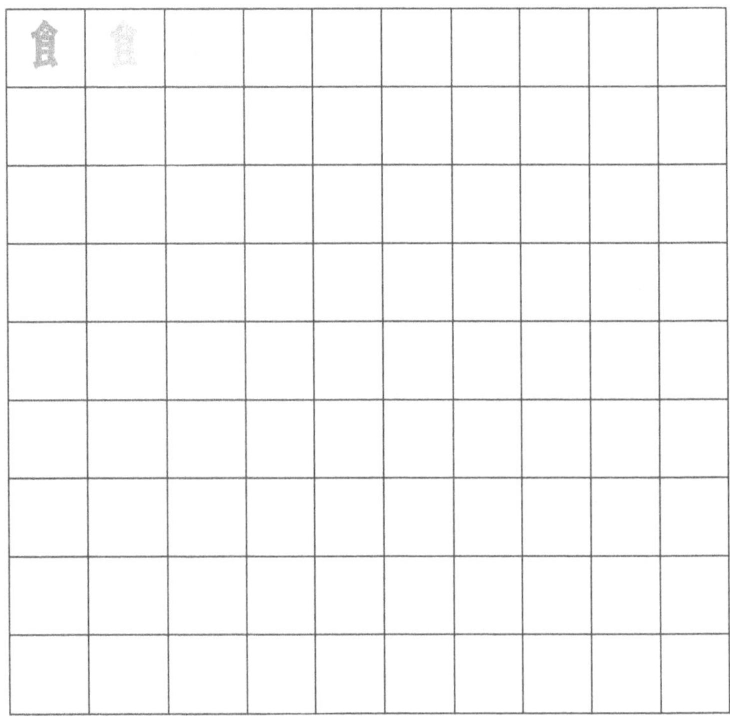

HORSE 馬

The radical for **"horse"** (馬) is a large, majestic component whose etymology is deeply intertwined with military strategy, transportation, and agricultural life. In a character, it almost always signals a theme of speed, physical strength, or the management of animals.

 Known in Japanese as **うま** (*uma*), this radical is one of the most recognizable "animal" sketches in the writing system. **The Top** represents the head and the flowing mane. **The four dots at the bottom** are the **four legs**. The final stroke on the right represents the horse's tail.

When 馬 appears, it usually steers the character into one of these three categories:

1. **Types and Breeds of Horses:**

    *   駒 (こま – colt/pony/chess piece): A **horse** (馬) that is "full/refined".

2. **Actions and Riding:**

    *   駐 (ちゅう – stop/station/park): A **horse** (馬) that is "staying" like a **pillar** (主).

3. **Surprise and Commotion:**

    *   驚 (おどろく – surprised/astonished): The feeling of a **horse** (馬) jumping in fright at a "command/respect" (敬).

HORSE

馬 馬 馬 馬 馬 馬 馬 馬 馬 馬

Try it:

DEMON 鬼

The radical for **"demon"** (鬼) holds a hauntingly unique position in Japanese culture. Known as **おに** (*oni*), it categorizes everything from malevolent spirits and magical forces to the deeply philosophical concepts of the human soul.

This radical is a literal "portrait" of a spirit. In ancient times, people believed that spirits were invisible, so they depicted them through ritual masks. The oversized, boxy top represents a terrifying **ritual mask** or the **grotesque face** of a spirit. The middle section depicts the **legs of a person**, showing that these spirits were once human. The little flick at the bottom represents the **supernatural** "extra" element.

When 鬼 appears, it pulls the character into the realm of the invisible or the extraordinary:

1. **Ghosts and Supernatural Beings:**

   - 魔 (ま –witch): It represents the unseen forces of the forest or the dark.

2. **Spiritual Characteristics and the Soul:**

   - 魂 (たましい–soul): A **spirit** (鬼) that floats away like a **cloud** (云).

3. **Abstract Behaviors and "Haunting" Traits:**

   - 魅 (み –bewitch): It describes a beauty so intense it feels supernatural or "haunting."

DEMON

鬼

Try it:

FISH 魚

The radical for **"fish"** (魚) is a vivid pictogram that demonstrates the ancients' observation and abstraction of aquatic life. It serves as the primary classifier for hundreds of different sea creatures, as well as the biological traits and culinary states associated with them.

Known in Japanese as **うお** (*uo*), this radical is a top-to-bottom map of a fish. The top slanted strokes represent the pointed snout or **head of the fish**. The central box represents **the scales and the main torso** of the fish. Finally, just like in the "Horse" radical, the four dots represent movement—in this case, the flickering of **fins and the tail** as the fish swims.

When 魚 appears, it anchors the character firmly in the maritime world:

1. **Specific Fish Species:**

   - 鯛 (たい – sea bream): A **fish** (魚) that is "round" or "circumferential" (周).

2. **Biological Characteristics and Behaviors:**

   - 鱗 (りん – scales): The "neighboring" (隣) parts of a **fish** (魚).

3. **Processing and State Description:**

   - 鮮 (せん – fresh): A combination of **fish** (魚) and **sheep** (羊). In ancient times, these two were the primary symbols of fresh, delicious food.

FISH

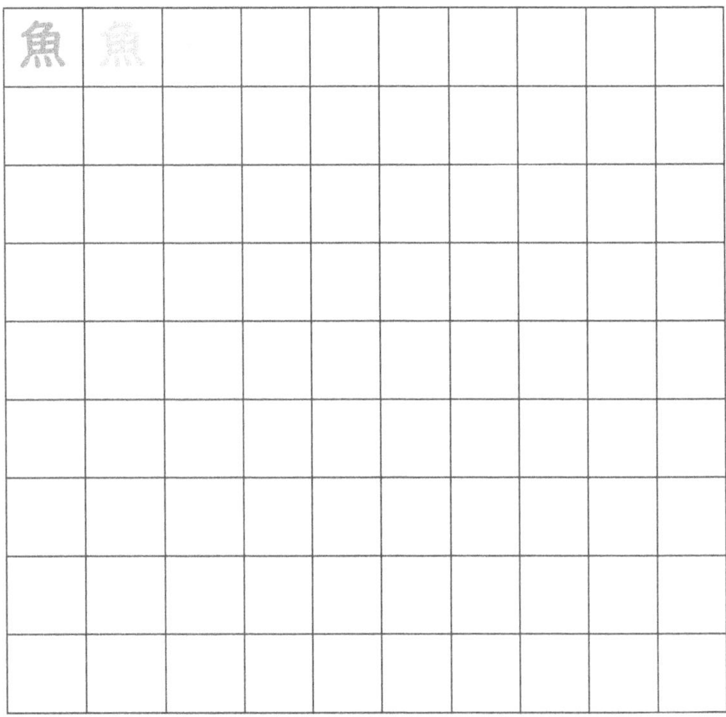

BIRD 鳥

The radical for **"bird"** (鳥) is a complex and systematic component. It doesn't just record the ecology of the ancient world; it reflects a specific classification logic. While 隹 represents small, perching birds, 鳥 is the go-to radical for larger birds, swimming birds, and those with prominent tails.

Known in Japanese as と り (*tori*), this radical is one of the most detailed pictograms in the Japanese language. The hooked stroke represents the **beak and head**. The boxy section represents the **eye and the body**. In ancient scripts, the eye was very prominent to show the bird's alertness. The four dots represent the **tail feathers** or the claws.

When 鳥 appears, it usually flies into one of these two categories:

1. **Specific Bird Names:**

   - 鶏 (にわとり – chicken): A "tame" bird found in the "valley."

   - 鶴 (つる – crane): A bird (鳥) that is of "high ambition". A symbol of longevity in Japan.

2. **Characteristics and Size:**

   - 鴻 (こう – large bird): It implies something grand or socially significant.

BIRD

鳥 | 亻 | 户 | 户 | 鳥 | 鳥 | 鳥 | 鳥 | 鳥 | 鳥 | 鳥

Try it:

RADICAL LIST TABLE

RADICAL	NOMBRE	CONCEPT & EXAMPLES
一	ONE	**Unity & Foundations:** 上 (Up) 下 (Down)
亠	LID	**Generic Covers:** 京 (Capital) 亡 (Deceased)
人 亻	PERSON	**Human Traits:** 休 (Rest) 体 (Body)
儿	LEGS	**Human Stance:** 先 (Before) 兄 (Big Brother)
八	EIGHT	**Separation:** 公 (Public) 具 (Tool)
冖	COVER	**Enclosure:** 冠 (Crown) 冥 (Dark)
冫	ICE	**Coldness:** 冷 (Cold) 凍 (Freeze)
刀 刂	KNIFE	**Cutting Actions:** 切 (Cut) 刻 (Cut fine)

RADICAL	NOMBRE	CONCEPT & EXAMPLES
力	FORCE	**Effort:** 勉 (Exert) 功 (Merit)
十	TEN	**Completion:** 千 (Thousand) 南 (South)
卩	SEAL	**Authority:** 印 (Stamp) 即 (Immediate)
厂	CLIFF	**Geography:** 厚 (Thick) 厄 (Calamity)
又	RIGHT HAND	**Repetition:** 取 (Take) 友 (Friend)
口	MOUTH	**Speaking/Eating:** 味 (Flavor) 叫 (Shout)
口	ENCLOSURE	**Containment:** 国 (Country) 囚 (Prisoner)
土	SOIL	**Ground:** 地 (Ground) 城 (Castle)
夕	EVENING	**Time:** 夢 (Dream) 外 (Outside)

RADICAL	NOMBRE	CONCEPT & EXAMPLES
大	BIG	**Size:** 天 (Heaven) 太 (Fat)
女	WOMAN	**Family:** 姉 (Older sister) 妹 (Younger sister)
子	CHILD	**Beginnings:** 学 (Study) 孫 (Grandchild)
宀	ROOF	**Household:** 家 (Home) 安 (Cheap)
寸	MEASURE	**Small Precision:** 導 (Guide) 専 (Specialty)
小	SMALL	**Size:** 少 (Few) 当 (To hit)
尸	CORPSE	**Living/Dead:** 居 (Reside) 尿 (Urine)
辶	ROAD	**Travel & Movement:** 道 (Road) 速 (Fast)
山	MOUNTAIN	**Nature & Elevation:** 岩 (Rock) 峠 (Mountain pass)

RADICAL	NOMBRE	CONCEPT & EXAMPLES
工	CRAFT	**Construction:** 左 (Left) 差 (Difference)
巾	CLOTH	**Fabric & Hanging:** 布 (Cloth) 帳 (Notebook)
广	BUILDING	**Large Buildings:** 庁 (Government office) 広 (Wide)
弓	BOW	**Flexibility & War:** 引 (Pull) 強 (Strong)
彡	HAIR	**Pattern & Flow:** 形 (Shape) 影 (Shadow)
彳	GOING	**Human Movement:** 後 (After) 従 (Obey)
幺	SMALL THREAD	**Smallness:** 幼 (Young) 幽 (Faint)
心 忄	HEART	**Emotions:** 怖 (Scary) 忘 (Forget)
戈	HALBERD	**Warfare:** 成 (Become) 戦 (War)

RADICAL	NOMBRE	CONCEPT & EXAMPLES
戸	DOOR	**Household:** 戻 (Return) 扇 (Fan)
手扌	HAND	**Physical Tasks:** 打 (Hit) 技 (Skill)
攵	STRIKE	**Forceful Action:** 教 (Teach) 政 (Government)
方	DIRECTION	**Orientation:** 旅 (Trip) 於 (At)
斤	AXE	**Chopping:** 断 (Cut off) 新 (New)
日	SUN	**Time/Light:** 明 (Bright) 晴 (Clear weather)
月	MOON	**Cycles:** 有 (Exist) 期 (Period)
木	WOOD	**Wood:** 桜 (Sakura) 机 (Desk)
欠	LACK	**Empty/Breath:** 歓 (Delight) 欲 (Want)

RADICAL	NOMBRE	CONCEPT & EXAMPLES
止	STOP	**Stationary:** 歩 (Walk) 歳 (Age)
歹	DEATH	**Endings:** 死 (Death) 残 (Remain)
殳	WEAPON	**Force:** 段 (Step) 殺 (Kill)
水 氵	WATER	**Liquids & Flow:** 池 (Pond) 泳 (Swim)
牛	COW	**Livestock & Sacrifice:** 牲 (Sacrifice) 牧 (Pasture)
犬 犭	DOG	**Animals:** 猫 (Cat) 狩 (Hunt)
火 灬	FIRE	**Heat & Energy:** 燃 (Burn) 焦 (Scorch)
王	KING	**Authority & Value:** 理 (Justice) 珠 (Pearl)
田	RICE PADDY	**Agriculture/Logic:** 町 (Town) 男 (Man)

RADICAL	NOMBRE	CONCEPT & EXAMPLES
疒	ILLNESS	**Illness:** 病 (Sick) 疲 (Be tired)
皿	DISH	**Vessels:** 盆 (Tray) 盗 (Steal)
目	EYE	**Vision:** 盲 (Blind) 眺 (View)
石	STONE	**Hard Objects:** 岩 (Rock) 砲 (Cannon)
示 礻	ALTAR	**Rituals:** 祝 (Celebrate) 神 (God)
禾	GRAIN	**Staple Foods:** 秋 (Autumn) 税 (Tax)
穴	HOLE	**Empty Space:** 空 (Sky/Empty) 窓 (Window)
立	STANDING	**Stature:** 競 (Compete) 端 (Edge)
竹	BAMBOO	**Crafts/Paper:** 筆 (Brush) 箸 (Chopsticks)

RADICAL	NOMBRE	CONCEPT & EXAMPLES
米	RICE	**Nutrition:** 粉 (Powder) 粗 (Coarse)
糸	THREAD	**Connection:** 線 (Line) 結 (Tie)
罒	NET	**Entrapment:** 罪 (Crime) 置 (Place)
羊	SHEEP	**Goodness/Wool:** 群 (Flock) 美 (Beauty)
羽	FEATHER	**Flight:** 習 (Learn) 翌 (Next)
肉 月	FLESH	**Body Parts:** 肌 (Skin) 背 (Back)
舟	BOAT	**Watercraft:** 航 (Sail) 船 (Ship)
⺾	GRASS	**Vegetation:** 花 (Flower) 芋 (Potato)
虫	INSECT	**Creatures:** 蚊 (Mosquito) 蛇 (Snake)

RADICAL	NOMBRE	CONCEPT & EXAMPLES
衣衤	CLOTHING	**Textiles & Apparel:** 袖 (Sleeve) 裝 (Attire)
耳	EAR	**Hearing:** 聽 (Listen) 職 (Employment)
虎	TIGER	**Majesty & Danger:** 虐 (Oppress) 虜 (Captive)
行	JOURNEY	**Movement:** 術 (Art) 衛 (Defense)
見	SEE	**Observation:** 規 (Rule) 親 (Parent)
言	SPEECH	**Communication:** 評 (Critique) 詩 (Poem)
貝	SHELL	**Value & Commerce:** 買 (Buy) 財 (Wealth)
足	FOOT	**Movement:** 路 (Road) 踏 (Step)
車	CAR	**Transportation:** 輪 (Wheel) 輸 (Transport)

RADICAL	NOMBRE	CONCEPT & EXAMPLES
邑	TOWN	Settlement: 都 (Capital) 郊 (Suburbs)
酉	ALCOHOL	Fermentation: 酒 (Sake) 酢 (Vinegar)
金	METAL	Wealth/Tools: 銀 (Silver) 針 (Needle)
門	GATE	Passageways: 開 (Open) 閣 (Tall building)
阜	MOUND	Geography: 阪 (Slope) 降 (Descend)
隹	SMALL BIRD	Perching: 集 (Gather) 雀 (Sparrow)
雨	RAIN	Weather: 雲 (Cloud) 電 (Electricity)
頁	HEAD	Intelligence: 顔 (Face) 類 (Category)
食	FOOD	Sustainability: 飯 (Meal) 飲 (Drink)

RADICAL	NOMBRE	CONCEPT & EXAMPLES
馬	HORSE	**Power/Speed:** 驚 (Surprise) 駒 (Pony)
鬼	DEMON	**Spiritual:** 魂 (Soul) 魅 (Charm)
魚	FISH	**Sea:** 鮮 (Fresh) 鯛 (Sea bream)
鳥	BIRD	**Avian:** 鶴 (Crane) 鶏 (Chicken)

Beyond the Strokes: The Journey Continues

You have just mastered 93 of the most vital building blocks in the Japanese language. What once looked like a chaotic maze of lines and dots has now become a collection of stories, tools, and symbols. By understanding these radicals, you haven't just memorized shapes—you've learned to see the world through the eyes of the ancients.

This book was designed to be your map, making the daunting peak of Kanji feel like a manageable, and even joyful, ascent. But remember: a map is only useful if you keep walking.

The world of Japanese is vast, but you no longer stand at the gates—you have the keys to open them.

Let's Keep the Conversation Going

The journey of learning a language is never meant to be traveled alone. If you want to dive deeper, share your progress, or if you simply hit a wall and need a hand to pull you up, come find me!

 Join the Community:
@JLPTKanjiMnemonics

Ask & Engage: I'm always active in the comments and DMs, ready to answer your questions and celebrate your wins: **jlptkanjimnemonics@gmail.com**

The strokes end here, but your story with Japanese is just beginning. Let's make it legendary.

ありがとうございます

www.ingramcontent.com/pod-product-compliance
Lightning Source LLC
Chambersburg PA
CBHW060915140726
47996CB00001B/260